Happiness
You Are the Author of Your Life!

By: Peter Tassi

CONTENTS

PREFACE

Our society promotes the material life with the illusion that material things, power, popularity, and instant gratification will promote a state of happiness. These things do not promote true happiness and the happiness they do provide are only moments of happiness. Moments are only moments. What exists between them is unhappiness.

Don't settle for unhappiness!

You are the author of your life and your own happiness. Don't let others mislead you. Free yourself of what small-minded people think and find to be true happiness. You deserve it!

The formula for happiness and the path to find it is offered to you in this body of work. My discoveries were made based on research, reflection and the influence and inspiration of so many great and wonderful people. My struggle to find the path to happiness was brought to the forefront many times throughout my career as an educator, chaplain, mission worker and counsellor to many students and staff. Often, in these sessions, I sought answers to alleviate their suffering and provide them with a path for happiness. This, combined with my own personal journey, served as a powerful motivation to walk the pilgrimage.

PROMISES

To guarantee a meaningful, purpose-filled happy life, you will make three promises to yourself. This may sound frightening, setting yourself up for failure, but this is not the case. Unlike a New Year's Eve promise, these are covenants reflecting who you truly are.

By making promises that reflect who you truly are, you will be more committed to the promises, and more willing to make the journey to actualize these promises. You will, in fact, be creating a path to living the life you were called to live; and in so doing, have a happy life.

As soon as the word "promises" is mentioned, one may think of all those New Year's resolutions that they made and broke; or one may think of the promises made regarding their work or relationship which they failed to keep. Consequently, the word "promise" may bring with it a host of bad feelings and memories of failures; but I don't want you to think of promises in this way.

I want you to think of promises made as they relate to the person you want to become. I want you to think of how sacred and wonderful promises are and how they propel you to become a better person living the moral life. I want you to think of the most beautiful moments in your life when you made promises that had to do with your own personal development at becoming a better person. Don't think of failures.

Focus on how renewed you felt, determined to embark on a new path that was to bring fulfillment and joy. Focus on how these promises strengthened you to be a better person and live a more flourishing life.

The promises you will make to yourself, for the sake of

achieving happiness, are promises that reflect who you actually are, rather than promises about changing habits. In this way, they exist as part of you, rather than being external promises like,

"I promise to go the gym five days a week."

The promises you make here have to do with *who you actually are* and in this way they are important life-changing promises. Although fulfilling these promises will involve challenges and difficulties, you will be committed to them and in spite of possible setbacks, you will be unwilling to give up on yourself.

I want you to make these promises to yourself. These are promises that will enrich your life and lead you to living a more meaningful and purpose-filled life; promises that have to do with *who you are*, rather than what you are going to do.

Your actions and the life you live will follow, after you become the person you are called to be. You can promise to be a better listener for your spouse but if you have not changed who you actually are, you will fail. I want you to make these new promises because they will change the person you are and will result in you living a moral and virtuous life. This will bring you happiness.

We will be looking at these three promises, which you will make to yourself. Don't be anxious or afraid. These three promises will be made clear, and the path will be laid out for you in this book. You will be guided throughout your journey.

Focus on the finishing line and on winning the ultimate prize: happiness, contentment, and living a rich life filled with purpose and meaning.

These promises you will make to yourself are actually

covenants. We see this concept in the Judeo-Christian tradition describing the relationship between God and his people. These covenants between Yahweh and the Israelite's were promises with an added dimension. Covenants were made between Yahweh and Abraham, Moses, David, and Noah. In each case, Yahweh would deliver on his promise and the Israelite's were expected to deliver on their promise.

What made these promises more than just a contract or an agreement, was that they were unconditional and forever.

They had no expiry date or loopholes to escape the agreement. They were also unconditional in that failure to meet one's end of the bargain did not terminate the relationship. This is what makes covenant much more than an agreement or contract.

This is the kind of promise or covenant you will be making to yourself in your pursuit of happiness. At times, you may fail. At times, you may fall back to the old self, but you will forgive yourself and move forward. In spite of the ups and downs, the misgivings, and failures, you will hold true to these promises you made to yourself. You will forgive yourself and start anew, moving forward in your pursuit of happiness.

To live a flourishing life filled with meaning and purpose and attain true happiness, you will begin your journey by making these three promises to yourself.

First, you promise to empty yourself of the person you were, so that you can receive the revelations that will fill you with truth, and allow you to become the person you were meant to be.

Second, you promise to live this new you, founded on truth, to become the person of love that truth calls you to be.

4

Third, you promise to put this new you, a person of love founded on truth, into motion through living out **Eight Key Virtues**, as explained in Chapter10,"REFORMATION." This is the covenant you will make with yourself, and by fulfilling this covenant, you will find and live true happiness.

When we look at promise number one, the promise may be misleading if you read it purely from a western point of view. The notion of "completely emptying yourself of the person you are," may suggest that you get rid of the good aspects of your character. We don't want you to do that. When we look at this concept from an eastern perspective, we empty ourselves of who we are, with the understanding that when we become the new person, reflecting the divine within, we never lose those purely good, life-giving qualities that we had.

Regarding the second promise, it is our very nature to love and to be beings of love. This is the truth that we discover; that we are, at our core, beings of love. In essence, we have to work at being who we truly are, and know that any variation of living out that calling will lead to unhappiness.

Our third promise is made on the knowledge that becoming this being of love, will affect all our thoughts, intentions, and deeds. You will also recognize the importance of the eight key virtues, and their integral role in helping you to embody this life of love that is expressed through these virtues. Expression of the third promise can be fulfilled in all aspects of life—even with your quite thoughts as you lay motionless in bed.

Although we still have work to do before we start our pilgrimage, let's state again our **three promises**.

1."I promise to empty myself of the person I was, so that I can receive the revelations that will fill me with truth.

2. I promise to live this new me, founded on truth, and become the person of love that truth calls me to be.

3. I promise to put this new me—a person of love, founded in truth—into motion, through living out the eight key virtues."

THE BEGINNING

Like everyone, I sought happiness. The search began as a young teenager. Even at that age I was asking the philosophical questions. I wanted to understand what exactly happiness was and what kind of life it would lead one to pursue or follow.

Throughout my life, I found myself so busy with career, interests, hobbies and raising a family, I didn't spend enough time exploring and pursuing happiness. I was too busy to find happiness. Consequently, I often suffered unhappiness.

There were times I gave it serious reflection, especially as a counselor for those who suffered much. Eventually, the suffering of the many students and staff I counselled, the suffering of the hundreds of the poor I met in the Developing World and the suffering I experienced in my own life drove me to find the answer to human suffering. It drove me to discovering how one finds happiness.

It wasn't just their suffering that served as a catalyst that drove me to find the secret to happiness, it was also their happiness. I marvelled at those I counseled who lived in miserable conditions, bore a horrendous past life and, even in the midst of their present conditions, they found happiness. I was inspired by those in the Third World who lived in misery but chose not to be miserable. I desperately sought the answer to the question, "How could one have suffered such as these people and have found happiness in spite of their suffering?"

Like the Hindu, who in the fourth stage of life seeks spiritual liberation, I returned to a more serious reflection, in depth research, and my own personal pilgrimage to find true happiness. As a result of my discoveries and awareness, I present this work. The approach is theologically ecumenical and involves philosophical and psychological thought. The discovery is unique, and although universal, it is a personal enlightenment.

The definition and path is clear and simple. This path will present you with challenges, but you will overcome them in your pursuit of your own happiness.

I do not claim that this is the only path—there are many.

Since the ancient Greeks, great minds have been writing about this complex topic and offering theories, definitions, and formulas. Christianity, Buddhism, and many of the great religions offer a way of life that is happiness. Only you can decide the path that is best for you. I am confident that the path offered here will serve you well in your pursuit for happiness.

GENESIS

The most peace-filled, content, and happy man I ever met was my father. Yet, he suffered from bouts of depression. I was just a teenager and during one such bout I asked him if he was okay. He was well aware of my worry, and he replied, "Don't worry son, someone can be depressed and be very happy."

It confused me. I didn't understand what it meant, but it stuck with me throughout my life. I continued to reflect on it.

Decades passed, and while working at Mother Theresa's "House of Malnutrition and Dying" one of the Sisters shed light on this mystery. I spoke with her about the difficult work she did in the most deplorable and pain-filled environment. I asked her why she would choose this life over a more comfortable and pleasant life in my country. She answered, "Although my work and life is uncomfortable and involves great suffering, I am happy. Doing what God has called me to do brings me great joy."

Throughout my youth I would have occasional existential questions, asking myself, "How does one achieve happiness?

Where else for a young guy like me to go with such a question but to my father; a profound, humble man of few words.

I asked him, "Dad, how does one achieve happiness?" He simply answered, "Keep your head cool, your feet warm with lots of blank pages in between." As usual, rather dumbfounded by his answer, I buried it in the recess of my mind for reflection at another time. It wasn't any one statement my father said that led to the realization I share with you in this book. It was an accumulation of years of listening to him and watching him live his life of love.

More important than the research I began to do, I reflected on all the great people I met throughout my life and careers. Then it came to me. Happiness equals Truth plus Love plus Motion. One arrives at this place through a three-step journey, Reception, Realization and Reformation. To start such a daunting journey, one must make promises to oneself. Promises that will help them see the journey through to the end. Promises that, in spite of our own frailties and failings, we will not give up on, during our pursuit for happiness. Promises that are, in themselves, the embodiment of happiness.

HAPPINESS

Do whatever it takes to find happiness, no matter how much suffering it involves. – P.T.

I think it is safe to say that we all want happiness. St. Augustine said, "Everyone, whatever his condition, desires to be happy. There is no one who does not desire this, and each one desires it with such earnestness that it is preferred to all other things; whoever in fact, desires other things, desires them for this end alone."

We desire happiness because it is fundamental to our being. It is necessary to live a full, rich life. Jesus, the Buddha, and other great religious leaders recognized this, so, they offered a path to happiness and wanted us to be happy. We deserve happiness by the nature of our humanity.

For the theist who believes that we are created in God's image with infinite wisdom, beauty and love, happiness is certainly deserving to such a person. Also, the non-believer, who believes that at our core we are good, as is the premise of this work, deserves happiness. And, therefore, this happiness is awarded and deserving to all who live the *good life*, the life of goodness.

In spite of all this, happiness often eludes us. We desire and deserve it and yet, we have difficulty achieving it. Why is that? If we want it, deserve it and it is a primary driving force, why is it so difficult to find happiness? There are many theories to explain why happiness is hard to find. Some theories state that it cannot be found, and we have to live our lives short of true happiness. Some will say that the journey is too long and hard, and we should learn to be content in our discontent. Others claim that happiness is genetic, reserved for only those born with the happy gene.

Many make the claim that living a full, happy life is not possible—that only moments of happiness are possible.

Some claim that if you try to pursue it, you lose it before you start.

In other words, it is not an object that can be pursued, only a state that can be lived. It is the premise of this book that we can all find happiness and that happiness can become our way of life. In fact, not only is finding happiness achievable, but we also have a moral responsibility to find it. To live a happy life –truly happy- is not only good for self, but also for all others in our life. And, paradoxically, living a life that is good for others, is what happiness is!

If you are able to do good for others, you have a moral responsibility to do so. Ironically, as you will see in this book, it is by doing good for others, that we achieve true happiness. All of us have the ability to be a person for others: for our partner, children, siblings, family, and the global community. We have this ability because it is who we are, at the core of our being.

Happiness makes us complete, and results in living a flourishing life, bringing out the very best in us. By being happy, and living a flourishing life, we will impact positively on others, not only because happiness is intrinsically connected to service, as we will later see, but also because happiness is infectious and brings out the very best in ourselves and those with whom we come in contact. It is impossible to be the best we can be, and do the best we can do for others, if we are not happy.

I offer my discovery to you in humility and yet, at the same time, I am so bold as to say that it is true. The formula is:

Happiness = Truth + Love + Motion.

This is the simple definition of happiness: acquiring truth plus being a person of love plus putting love into motion.

One discovers truth, becomes a person of love, and puts this love into motion through a three-step pilgrimage: Reception, Realization and Reformation.

Before starting your pilgrimage, do not allow what appears to be simple, lead you to believe that you will not be confronted with obstacles and challenges. For this reason, this self-pilgrimage must be more than just a decision for you, it must involve promises you make to yourself. Promises or *covenants* that are everlasting, standing the test of difficulty and time. Promises that you will pursue truth, that you will be a person of love and that you will put this love into motion through the eight virtues.

"No pain, no gain." The paradox of life is that joy and suffering, victory and defeat, life and death are each two sides of the same coin. To fulfill the promises and find your own happiness you have to give up all that you are, to become all that you should be. You have to give up ego, self-pity, misery, momentary gratifications, darkness, and ignorance. You have to shed preconceived ideas, prejudices, bitterness, anger, and resentments. We all have the ability to achieve clear mindedness (receive truth), be kind-hearted (live love) and live this life (put into motion). We have the ability to do it and we are called to do it because it is who we are. You will embody this new person, a person who acquires and lives truth, a being of love who lives a life, demonstrated through the eight virtues, that exemplifies this new you.

You must make the decision that what you want is true happiness and that you are willing to endure the pilgrimage. Guess what? **YOU CAN DO IT!** Happiness is within reach and as difficult as the journey may be, it will be filled with wonder and awe.

Some people have been subject to one misfortune after another and are subject to having to live a life of hardship, at no fault of their own, yet they still find happiness. They did not use hardship as an excuse to neglect their duty to find happiness.

Many of the people I have met in my life, including the ones I counselled, from youth to middle aged, had found happiness in the most difficult of situations. Amazingly, many of the street kids I worked with, as dissatisfied as they were with their economic situation and poor living conditions, were very happy youth. Many were happier than the youth from wealthy families, who were living the privileged life. This teaches us that although our life may be shaped by undesirable circumstances, we still remain in control of our approach and attitude towards such a life, and of the kind of life we choose to live. And so it is with happiness; we are in control, and no situation or person can deter us from finding truth, becoming a person of love, and putting our new life into motion.

The famous boxer, James Braddock, faced what appeared to be an unbeatable foe, when he fought Max Baer for the heavyweight championship of the world. Braddock was old and beaten up and Max Baer was young, viscous and a killer in the ring. You may remember the words the crowd shouted out to him before the fight began; "You can do it Jimmy." And, do it he did, defeating Baer in a decision. These same words I say to you: **YOU CAN DO IT!"**

THE PATH

"The greatest explorer on this earth never takes voyages as long as those of the man who descends to the depth of his heart." – Julien Green

Any path that leads to something significant will be difficult. Think of successful people, great athletes prophets of our time. They did not come by their accomplishments easily. It was hard work. The great philosophers, theologians and people who have achieved enlightenment, came by it with hard work.

I once asked my father, who I believed to have achieved enlightenment, a state of total peace and happiness, "How did you become the person you are and achieve your state of mind?" He simply answered, "Hard work." It would be a false premise if I was to tell you that this journey within will be an easy one. The journey within is the most difficult journey one can take.

Happiness is accomplished by reaching the Core of your being and becoming one with the Divine, one with your true nature. Happiness is impossible if we live a life that does not reflect who we truly are. We have to be who we are, to be content. And who are we? We must live truth, become beings of love that truth calls us to be, and put this truth and love into motion.

That is what we are at our Core: truth and love put into motion. To find and become that person we embark on this journey. This journey will involve travelling through three steps:

Reception of Truth, Realization of Love and Reformation of Life. Through this journey, we will come to actualize who we truly are and actualize what happiness is.

15

Happiness = Truth + Love + Motion.

Many of the great religions and modern prophets agree that it is at our Core that we discover our true nature. And, by becoming who we are, we achieve happiness. The great religions and modern prophets all challenge us to make this journey within. I offer you, in this book, a road map to this place. We make three promises to ourselves, reflected in the three-step journey, revealing your path to happiness:

1. We put ourselves into a state of mind and heart so that
we can RECEIVE revelations to know TRUTH.

2. These truths help us REALIZE who we truly are: beings of LOVE.

3. We are REFORMED into people founded on truth, cloaked in love and we put this into MOTION through the virtues.

Some ask, "Can we find perfect happiness?"

Because we are human, it may not be perfect happiness or a perfect life, but it is what I would call *complete happiness* and a *complete life*. It could be argued that even Jesus, the Buddha, Lau Tzu, Gandhi, and other great people, never achieved perfect happiness. We live in a body and mind that is frail and a world that is imperfect.

However, we can argue that these people found what I would call complete happiness, the happiness found by being the person they were created to be. In this way, as described by the formula herein, we live with complete happiness.

Confucius said, "The man who conquers a thousand armies is great, the man who conquers himself is greater." He is greater because he endured the most difficult of journeys. This person went through the fire and endured the suffering it entailed. In our society, and one may argue, in any society since the beginning of civilization, suffering has been a dirty word. In fact, we do all we can to avoid suffering. If you want to build character, win over yourself, and find happiness, you must be willing to endure suffering.

The human heart is love, our true nature, and we cannot avoid this. The more we avoid this for the sake of avoiding discomfort or suffering, the more miserable we will be. Suffering is not an obstacle to happiness. It is the ingredient necessary to attain happiness. In fact, it is intrinsically connected to happiness. The key is not to avoid suffering but to learn how to suffer.

We should not find comfort in dealing with our own suffering by comparing ourselves with those worse off, or by focusing on the glass half-full. Nor should we view suffering as the gateway to heaven, as the punishment for sins or the price to pay for being a disciple. We have to look at suffering as a gift that will bring truth, humility, discernment, and compassion to our being and to the lives of others. This is the paradox of life. We should be thankful for our suffering, and rather than running from it, embrace it.

This may sound like a rather radical approach to suffering but, as you will see, we must embrace suffering to find true happiness. Suffering must become our friend and our companion. We have to breathe it in and out, allowing it to be the very fabric of the life we live. Embrace it, sleep with it, and even love it. If your present life is so dark that you cannot see this, be patient with yourself and you will see it. Be patient as you struggle out of your darkness. You will see that suffering can be your great companion. This does not mean that you seek out suffering. What I am saying, is that suffering is a natural part of our lives, and the more we can embrace it as our friend, the more we will find freedom from it.

If we can approach suffering in this way, we will view it as our ally in finding happiness. It will allow us to surrender, putting ourselves into the hands of truth and love, our inner nature. If we want complete happiness, we must be willing to accept a complete life, and this life will involve suffering.

Work to embrace that which is uncomfortable. Work at accepting and embracing the suffering, the very thing that will forge greatness within and bring true freedom.

Spending boundless energy and finding ways to escape suffering for the sake of comfort, will only imprison you to the escape, and atrophy your soul. One of my father's favourite four letter words was "duty." He sometimes asked me, "Why don't I hear people talking about doing their duty? I know that doing your duty involves sacrifice and sometimes suffering, but don't they realize the joy that comes with living such a life?"

Be filled with hope, remain determined, and the treasure awaits your arrival. Be patient with yourself, as you slowly become a person living in the knowledge of truth, cloaked in love, and putting into motion the new person you are becoming.

You will become an agent of change, healing the brokenness in others, and elevating them to higher ground. This is what your core calls you to be, and by becoming who you truly are, you live life to its fullness and find true happiness.

You will enjoy this journey. It will open for you a whole new world, where you will discover hidden treasures. You will discover just how beautiful a person you are. You will discover the power of your love. You will become a person of truth and love, and your life will exemplify this. Colleagues, family, friends, and employers will be astonished and inspired by your good character. You will become much more than just personality; you will become a truly great person, who impacts greatly on the lives of others.

H=TLM

"True religion is real living, living with all one's soul, with all one's goodness and righteousness."
– Albert Einstein

Socrates, Plato, and Aristotle, were three great Greek philosophers in the 3rd and 4th century B.C. Their work laid the groundwork for western philosophy, theology, and political systems. Aristotle claimed that the supreme good for humans is to look at their end purpose or goal: that goal or supreme good being happiness. This end goal will give our life meaning, because happiness is profound and enduring, allowing us to live our life according to our essential nature as rational beings. This happiness depends on the cultivation of virtue. To attain happiness, you must have moral character: complete virtue. Happiness is not virtue, but the exercise of virtue through reason, the exercise of virtue put into action. Plato's corresponding philosophy was that those who are moral are truly happy.

To live a full and flourishing human life we must be fully human: we must be who we were created to be; we must be who we truly are. Because happiness is our primary driving force and our greatest goal, it is our mission to travel to the Core of our being to discover what it means to be fully human. There are different definitions for the Core. Philosophers, psychologists, and religious leaders have all wrestled with the nature and substance at the core of our being. Many describe the Core as the place of consciousness where we find thought and feeling.

Others speak of it as the moral aspect or conscience of the person: our mental, moral, and emotional nature. Some refer to it as the heart of the person, and others as the essence of a person.

Many, who consider themselves spiritual, speak of it as the place where God is found. It is where we find the Divine. It is the place within where real-life exists and truth resides. To be fully human is to be one with the Core: Christ-like for the Christian, or the Bodhi-nature for the Buddhist. This Christ-like nature is to be a person of **TRUTH**, clothed in **LOVE** and this new person put into **MOTION**.

This is happiness: **H=TLM**.

To actualize this, we will fulfill the three promises by going through the three steps in this pilgrimage. We will empty ourselves so that we will have clear mindedness.

With this clear- mindedness, we will receive truth.

This truth will reveal that we are to live a life of love because this is who we truly are. And we will put this kind-heartedness into motion, through exercising the eight virtues in all that we think and do.

Throughout our lives, we experience many inspirations and revelations. They come to us almost on a daily basis.

We must always be in a state of RECEPTION to receive these inspirations and revelations. If we are in a state of reception, we will recognize the TRUTHS that are revealed to us. These truths reveal many things to us on a cognitive, emotional, and spiritual level. These revelations bring us to the REALIZATION that, at our Core, we are called to be beings of LOVE. With the knowledge of truths, and by becoming a person of love, we have experienced a REFORMATION, and now we are ready to put this new person into MOTION. This motion is best expressed by the virtues we will have acquired.

When we have travelled through these three steps and have actualized this equation, we have arrived at our Core, the Divine within. We become fully human, and live the life of healing others, elevating them to a higher ground.

The major world religions challenge us to make a pilgrimage to the Core, where we become one with the Divine, with our true nature. In Hinduism they teach that there is one Great Power, and that is Brahman. They speak of a life pilgrimage through our four Wants: Wealth, Social Order, Sensory Pleasure and, eventually, Spiritual Liberation. They recommend the Four-Fold Path of Knowledge, Meditation, Devotion, and finally, Good Works.

The purpose of this path is to achieve oneness with the Divine within, thus achieving Moksha or Liberation. This is liberation from the ego, resulting in an experience of Oneness with the universe, with Brahman.

Buddhism teaches the Four Noble Truths: All of life is suffering: suffering is caused by selfish cravings; release from suffering is achieved by release from craving; release or Liberation to Oneness and Wholeness can be achieved by following the Eightfold Path. This path involves Right View, Right Intention, Right Speech, Right Action, Right Livelihood, Right Effort, Right Mindfulness and Right Concentration. By following the Eightfold Path, we empty ourselves completely of ego and discover within, our Bodhi nature. It is here that we experience Liberation and Enlightenment and Oneness of the universe.

Taoism promotes meditation as a path that leads to the discovery of the Tao. We return to the Tao by achieving a mystical union with the Tao and it is here that we discover the oneness of all things in the Tao. It is here that ego is abandoned, one has no set mind, and the mind of all people is his mind. It is the ultimate reality where it is completely empty and yet all things emerge from it. This is liberation and happiness.

Islam teaches the Five Pillars: Profession of faith that there is One God, living a life of prayer, almsgiving to the poor, fasting, and making the pilgrimage. These Five Pillars challenge us to abandon pride and ego in order to achieve Oneness with Allah, resulting in living a life of peace and harmony.

In Christianity we follow the Sermon on the Mount, and specifically the Beatitudes (Matthew 5:1-12), as a path to experiencing oneness with our Christ nature, and hence, oneness with the world. Jesus offers the formula for happiness. He teaches us, "Happy are those who are spiritually poor, those who mourn, those who are humble, those who do what God requires, those who are merciful to others, those who are pure in heart, those who work for peace, those who are persecuted for doing what God requires." It is here, in this place with Jesus, at the deepest recess of our being, that we see all people as our brothers and sisters. It is when we live this life of the Beatitudes, we become one with the Christ within, and we experience true happiness.

We see that with all these great religions there is this path to our inner self. This inner self is the Divine, that which is our true nature. Once we have come in contact with the divine and embrace it as who we truly are, we are lead to a state of Enlightenment. Our life is transformed, and we are committed to serving and healing others. We have found happiness.

In this new life, we realize and experience the oneness of all humanity. We realize that we are brothers and sisters in the same family. We become one with the alcoholic, the drug addict, the criminal, the saint, the sinner. It is with this new realization of our Oneness, that we are no longer able to sit back and tolerate injustice. We are propelled to respond.

We want to be interconnected, but society continues to pull us apart from each other. Society would rather sell their wares to us as individuals, in competition with each other.

Instability, competitiveness, and wars are where the money is made, but happiness is lost.

Our most treasured commodity is our freedom. Not only from a world that separates us, enslaves us, and manipulates us, but freedom from ourselves: freedom from our ego, from living a life that is self-serving. We live a new life of service, a life that is full, flourishing with meaning and happiness. We will have emptied ourselves of ego and pride. We will be free of entanglements and attachment to possessions. We will be filled with the Divine within. Our great gifts and inner beauty will be expressed through the loving and free beings we have become.

Through living this life, we are truly free and happy.

PAVING THE WAY

To fill our cup with happiness we must empty our cup of pride, conceit, and the beliefs we cling to. – P.T.

Remind yourself of your first promise: "I promise to empty myself of the person I was so that I can receive the revelations that will fill me with truth." It is an exciting journey, but prior planning is essential.

You are probably willing and ready to embark on your personal pilgrimage to the Core. You may be anxious to begin the three steps and actualize the formula. However, it is critical that you are prepared. First, you must clear the way and put yourself in the right place. Like the carpenter says, "Measure three times and cut once." The key to success, at whatever you do, is preparation.

We have to take measure of ourselves, over and over, and then we will be ready to 'cut'. As you already know, there will be sacrifice and suffering involved in this process of measuring and cutting before embarking on the journey. To get rid of the old and to be born anew, requires suffering. But, as we discussed, we will make suffering our friend, and in this way, it will be easier to endure.

You are challenged to overcome five obstacles. These obstacles are so much a part of who you are and the life you live it will be a challenge to free yourself from them. It may appear to be too daunting a task. But, it is not. Note what Thomas Merton wrote: "What a strange thing! In filling myself, I had emptied myself. In grasping things, I had lost everything. In devouring pleasure and joy, I had found distress in anger and fear."

We have to be motivated and have the courage to "let go."

True freedom is freedom from our ego, our past, our comforts, our fears, and social pressures. We are challenged to reject power, status, money, and pleasures that imprison us. We must find the strength to reject the person society has made us, so that we can become the person we are called to be, a person of truth and love, put into motion, as expressed through the virtues.

1.Ego

Ego gets stuck and will resist change. It tells us that where we are is where we ought to be—always right in our present position. It is guilty of the sins of pride and self righteousness.

Our ego leads to physical attachments, as well as emotional ones.

We cling to security, self-image, ideologies, and a conviction that we are always right. These attachments make us unhappy and yet we cling to them. We have to dismantle our ego, completely emptying ourselves, making it possible to receive truths and look at life in a whole new way.

We don't have to renounce career, property, family, other people, and the world, just our old self. We have to let go of faults and sins, memories and past injuries, our sadness, and sorrows.

Let go and follow with empty hands.

While in Africa, I asked the Africans why they had so much faith and why God was so much a part of their life. They held out their hands in the shape of a cup and said, "When your hands are full of things, there is no room for

God, but when your hands are empty, there is only room for God."

Every moment and every experience offers us an opportunity to choose anew. We don't have to make the choices we have made in the past. We are given opportunities every day to remain the person we are, or to become a better person. If we can clear away our ego, we will have emptied our self and made room for everything new. We will free ourselves of always of acting and thinking, and will have lots of room to fill with inspiring revelations and truths.

Any attachment to our self will get in the way. Our vanity, youth, looks, money, prestige, position, or power will get in the way. If we are obsessed with being the controller, which we have to be in order to hold on to these things, we will never be open to this new life. We will not be in a state of receiving revelations and truths and living a new life of love. We are to be a blank sheet of paper, allowing life to make its mark on us: like an empty box that can be filled with hope. We are to empty our self of ego and selfish desires to be receptive to any revelation of truth.

The student went to the Zen Master to learn all that the Master had to offer. The Zen Master offered the student a cup of tea, then kept pouring the tea, even as it overflowed onto the floor. When the student asked the Master why he continued to pour the tea, the Master explained that the student was like the cup in which nothing can be put in if it is already filled with "stuff." We fill our life with stuff and distractions not because they bring us happiness, but because they distract us from our unhappiness. They fill us and our time, so we do not have to be alone with ourselves.

Jesus challenges us in His words, "Give up all that you have and come follow me." He may not be speaking as much about giving up your home, career, and material possessions, although that is a choice some have made. He is certainly talking about giving up all that you have in terms of ego, pride, self righteousness, prejudices, opinions, so that you are empty and can now receive truth.

When we empty our self of our ego, we will receive every revelation in an existential way. We will examine what may have seemed like an insignificant event, in a profound way, propelling us to a deeper reality. These revelations of truths, be they small or great, tell us that there is more to one's life than the life one has been living. These truths will reveal who we truly are.

2. The Past

Attachments to past grudges, injuries, failures, and wounds enslave us, and prevent any positive future. A past that has caused resentments and anger must be resolved and erased, so that our past is not our future.

This sometimes involves going all the way back to our childhood and dealing with those lies told to us, like we will never 'measure up,' or that we are stupid. These false messages have left us insecure and filled with unresolved anger. The same holds true for our past experiences. We may have experienced loss, financial woes, divorce, betrayal, and illness. Rather than leading us to be resentful or filled with self-pity, these experiences of suffering can serve as revelations, making us a better person.

Unfortunately, many of the suffering experiences we have had lead us to self-pity, anger, resentment, bitterness and sometimes a poor self-image. All of these are entanglements and when we become attached to them, allowing them to define who we are and the life we live, we become imprisoned; freedom is impossible, new revelations slip by us, and happiness is unattainable.

I often walk the beautiful beach strip with friends. On one occasion, a friend of one of us joined us in the walk. For an hour he spoke badly of his ex-wife. He talked about how selfish she was, how terrible a wife and mother she had been and that she had made the divorce a greater nightmare than the marriage. Once he left, I asked my friend, "When did that fellow get divorced?"

I was expecting that it was recently, after spending a long life together. To my surprise, my friend told me that this guy had divorced over 20 years ago. In spite of the intervening decades, this man was filled with resentment, anger, bitterness, and hatred. He was a prisoner to his past, never being able to free himself to receive all the beautiful revelations and truths life offers.

If you are entangled with your past, do not despair. You can rid yourself of your past and all the emotions associated with it. If your past has caught up to you, and the painful experiences and the lies you have believed about yourself have led to failures, do not despair because you can change your future. You can turn it all around, having your failures serve as a starting point for the new you. Your past and your failures can serve as a humbling experience, spurring an emptying of self and leaving room to receive that which is true. Before beginning step one (Reception), begin to empty yourself of all those things that have been enslaving you.

3. Comforts

We have been taught to seek comfort and to avoid suffering at all costs. As we have discussed, we must adopt a new attitude that encourages us to welcome discomforts and embrace suffering. Suffering does not mean we cannot be happy. In fact, suffering can shape and mold us into a better person and provide a bright future.

Suffering is the price for re-birth. It is like the blacksmith's fire used to shape a piece of steel. We can forge a shovel or a sword. We can allow our suffering to build our character, or to make us negative and bitter. Our suffering can serve as a tool to make us empathetic and loving, or unforgiving and hateful. Suffering can bring us to our knees and make us humble, or cause us to become arrogant and hostile.

Comforts can make us stale, settling for being half the person we can be. Comforts can kill our motivation to accomplish great things, whereas, discomfort and suffering keeps us alert and always open to receiving new truths. This does not mean that we seek out discomfort and suffering, but that we embrace it when it comes.

The athlete strives to make himself uncomfortable. He pushes his body beyond its limits. The more pain and discomfort he creates the better athlete he becomes. He pushes himself to the point where he breaks down his muscles so that they can rebuild to be leaner and stronger.

A woman welcomes and embraces the discomfort of her pregnancy and desires the time of birth, knowing it will bring great suffering, but embedded in that very suffering is her ability to give life. Michelangelo, as with many great artists, not only invited, but created great discomfort for himself, knowing it necessary to produce a masterpiece. He did not compromise the sacrifices he had to make, spending five years on his back painting to the point of near blindness, to create the Sistine Chapel.

You must see this in your own life. You know that that the reward for a parent is greater when they are willing to sacrifice time, energy and all the love required for the sake of their children. You know the suffering you have to endure when you want to accomplish something wonderful.

Missionaries recognize that with every experience of suffering brought to them by an impoverished person or sick child, there is also a great revelation about the truth regarding the interconnectedness of humanity. Sister Vera works in the missions in Mexico. She would break down and cry as she spoke about the death of a child, or the suffering of a young one who had been abused. Her tears were tears of pain and suffering.

However, as her tears fell to the ground, she lived out oneness with all those children. You knew that she was truly blessed, for her pain was a result of her connection with those in the world she served. And yet, this oneness that brought so much pain, also brought her purpose, meaning and happiness. Her pain was intrinsically connected to her joy. Without pain, she could not and would not experience the level of joy she attained.

The Buddha claimed that his last meal of poisonous mushrooms was his best meal. What does this mean? How can such discomfort and suffering, in this case death, be the greatest of meals? Before your journey comes to an end, and you have found happiness, you will make some sense of this mystery. It is a profound mystery. On the surface, we have seen how suffering must be endured to accomplish wonderful things, but this concept must permeate every aspect of our life and being.

The paradox and mystery is that with happiness comes suffering and with suffering comes happiness. In the case of your pilgrimage, you will embrace discomfort and suffering, so that you can be born anew. At the end of this journey, you will have found and become one with your true self. In so doing, you will have found happiness.

4. Fear

Fear can be good. We should fear what will happen to our body when we abuse it, or fear what will happen to our minds when we pollute it. We should fear what will happen to our souls when we do not exercise good character. Being social beings and living in community, we should fear doing anything that would bring shame or bad feelings to self and family. However, we often fear what we shouldn't fear. This

31

gets in the way of our greatness. It impedes us on our journey to discover truths, live love, and put this new life of love into motion.

Mysteriously, some fear that which is good for them.

They fear success—professional or personal. They even fear being successful at finding happiness. Consequently, they sabotage any chance of it. They have great talent and work hard, but as soon as success presents itself, they destroy the opportunity.

They may fear success or happiness because they do not believe they are worthy, or it may be because they do not want the responsibility to which it is attached. Perhaps this is because they are not willing to face the truth that they are wonderful and great. They may still believe the lies fed to them from childhood that they are not capable or worthy of success or happiness.

Steven Pressfield says, "Most of us have two lives: the life we live, and the unlived life within us." Do not be afraid to live the life within. You deserve that life, and the happiness you will find.

Fear can motivate what we do from morning to night, sometimes even shaping what we dare to think. Before beginning your pilgrimage, try to overcome your fears: fear of being overwhelmed, fear of abandonment, fear of anxiety, fear of losing who you are, fear of proving them all wrong, fear of being great. Take time to do an inventory of your fears and make the conscious effort to let them go.

We are more willing to cross the Sahara on a camel, the mighty oceans in an unworthy vessel, and hunt in the most dangerous jungles than we are to spend a month in monastic prayer and self-reflection. One marvels that people have the courage to parachute out of an airplane, race a car 200 miles an hour, or participate in ultimate fighting, but will not spend three days in reflective prayer and meditation. We find it easier to confront the lion in the jungle than the lion within. We find it easier to take a leap out of a plane than to leap into the Core.

Don't be afraid of this journey. You do not want to be dead while you are still alive. Everything you discover will be beautiful. It will be enlightening and liberating. You will see the beauty and greatness within you. You will leave behind the lies told to you. You will embark on the journey of living a life of purpose and meaning. You will impact on the lives of others and leave a footprint of love. You will be instrumental in healing a broken world.

Walt Disney went to ten people with his idea and nine of them told him he was crazy. He knew then that he was on to something great. Jesus was told he was a heretic and a false prophet. He was rejected by the authorities in his own religion and abandoned by his friends, but he conquered his fears, carried out his mission and changed the world. Gandhi, Nelson Mandela, the Dali Lama are just a few great spiritual leaders who conquered their fears and changed the world.

Don't fear rejection because it probably means you're onto something great. Don't fear failure because it means you have learned what not to do. Don't fear suffering because it means you are being forged into greatness. Don't fear this journey inward because you deserve happiness.

5. Social Pressures

Be successful; make a lot of money; secure a well-paying job; buy an impressive home; have a fancy car; own as much as you can; accumulate as much as possible; look beautiful; buy whatever it takes to make yourself attractive looking; be seen at important events; associate with successful people; act appropriately to better your standing, be politically correct...the list goes on forever.

It starts when we are born and ends when we die, and can follow us all the way in between. If we succumb to it, we have never truly lived. Perhaps this is what my father was referring to when he gave his formula for happiness. Remember what he said? "Keep your feet warm, your head cool with blank pages in between." We were created to write our own biography and not have it dictated to us.

Our society promotes the material life with the illusion that material things, power, popularity, and instant gratification will promote a state of happiness. The problem is that these things only promote moments of happiness. These may be great moments of happiness, but they are not true happiness. In thinking they are, we seek more and more of those moments, to fill the time between them. Consequently, those moments turn into addictions. You are the author of your biography. Don't let others write it for you. Free yourself of what small-minded people tell you about happiness and the things they ask of you.

Social pressures create a chaotic life. You are told, "do this, don't do that, become this, become that, think this way and not that way, set this as your goal, think only these kinds of thoughts, live this kind of life." You become so entangled in what is expected of you that you are never open to receiving truths.

You shrug off inspiring revelations as nothing but distractions. You become everything but what you were created to be. In humility, take all things under consideration but in the end, be your own author. Do not be concerned about what others, even loved ones who mean well, want you to be. Be concerned with what your Core calls you to be. Be concerned with who you are called to be.

As a rather rebellious, high spirited and impulsive teen, I was advised by my father to be willing to compromise all things, except my integrity. Integrity!? I didn't even know what the term meant. Once again, another piece of advice I banked somewhere in the deepest recess of my brain. This was his way of advising me to always remain true to the person I was called to be. And, I'm sure that I would mature into the kind of man who would eventually discover what I was called to be. He believed that we are, at our core, all called to be clear-minded, kind-hearted, virtuous people.

We cannot be open to revelations and inspirations if we succumb to social pressures. The material and chaotic life brought on by these pressures poisons us with emotions like confusion, anger, and jealousy. Social pressures demand that we constantly measure ourselves and our worth against the success of another. This competitive attitude leads to destruction. One such destructive element is being jealous of what others have or of their state in life. Jealousy leads to anger and has sparked wars between nations. Jealousy isolates us from others, always seeing others in a competitive spirit. It is one of the main causes of loneliness and leads to depression.

It's very difficult to separate self from the external world. We are social beings that live in community, and it is our responsibility to serve the community. That is what we are called to do. However, at the same time, we realize that it is impossible to be happy when we become mere subjects to the whims of the world. There seems to be, amongst the great thinkers and spiritual leaders, the ability to be completely of this world and yet, completely removed from the world.

The Following is an exercise you may want to work on to assist you in overcoming the obstacles:

1. In all that I plan to do today, how can my ego get in the way of doing what is right? In what ways have my motives been shaped by my need for acceptance, attention, praise, and power?

2. What are some of the experiences and teachings from my past that impede on my ability to see truth and be truly free? What can I do today to free myself from those parts of my past that imprison me and prevent me from thinking and living truth and freedom?

3. Am I willing to be uncomfortable for a greater good? In what ways am I willing to embrace discomfort today so that I can mold myself into a better person?

4. How are my fears preventing me from being the person I was called to be? How can I, on this day, overcome my fear of rejection, failure and anxiety and begin my pilgrimage to finding truth, living love and being the person I was called to be?

5. What kind of social pressures do I experience that impede my growth? In what ways can I be fully human today, shaking off these social pressures and becoming the free and beautiful person I am?

Now that you have overcome these five obstacles (ego, the past, comforts, fear, and social pressures); you have paved the way; you are ready for step one. You are ready to embark on the journey to your Core that will result in your happiness. You are able to find happiness through your own effort. You will find the happiness you seek and deserve, and in so doing you will become the great person that resides within you.

Now, let's begin our journey with step one.

RECEPTION

"The journey of a thousand miles begins with one step." – Lao Tzu

My first promise: "I promise to empty myself of the person I was so that I can receive the revelations that will fill me with that which is true."

Don't interpret this to mean that you rid yourself of that which is good. Based on your preparation to date you will know what you have to be emptied of. At your Core you are good and because of that, goodness is intrinsically attached to you, and you will not discard it. Don't hesitate to empty yourself of all things, knowing that whatever is pure goodness will remain with you at your Core.

Socrates claims that wisdom lies in the recognition of ignorance. Knowing one's own ignorance is the most important knowledge to have. This knowledge allows for transformation through the acquisition of truth. Our loyalties, therefore, should be to truth and wisdom. When our loyalties are to truth and wisdom, we are willing to take on the suffering involved in abandoning the old and becoming the new. When our loyalty is to truth and wisdom, we approach and live life in humility.

Humans are innately adventurous. An infant will repeatedly crawl and fall, bumping his or her head many times. This courage and determination carries into standing, to view the new world from the upright position. The risk of injury does not deter the child from repeated attempts to crawl and walk because they are determined to explore. We see this drive for adventure and exploration in teenagers as well. To our utter fear and worry, teenagers will explore at every opportunity!

This insatiable appetite for adventure, combined with courage, carries into adulthood. We take risks and continue to explore through love and marriage, having children, embarking on careers, and moving to new places to explore new opportunities. It is quite impressive to see the lengths humans will go to satisfy their quest for adventure. It is this courageous mindset that puts us in the right place to live an adventurous life and to search within. It is this mindset that will welcome truths, even the painful ones.

We receive revelations throughout our life, revelations that can inspire and transform us. These revelations can be private revelations or those revealed to us through a higher source. We think of revelations as big events; when Jesus gave the Sermon on the Mount; when the Buddha delivered the four noble truths, when Moses received the Ten Commandments.

Not all revelations are history-changing events, but they can serve as a personal-changing event. We receive revelations in all shapes, forms, and sizes. But we are so insulated by the world we live in; we often fail to recognize them. We fail to see that these experiences come to us to transform us. These revelations reveal profound truths about ourselves and the world. They can come from a walk in the woods, the affection from a child, the suffering of another, a kind gesture or even through a traumatic experience.

To receive these revelations in a way that they can have their full, intended effect on us, we must be in the right state of mind. The right state of mind, combined with the faculty of reason, allows us to recognize that a revelation is revealing to us a wonderful truth. The faculty of reason involves having a critical mind, calling everything into question, without being cynical or skeptical. This is what we must do to recognize these revelations and find the truths they reveal.

The right state of mind requires one to empty oneself. We previously spoke about this. With an emptying of self, combined with rational thought, we are able to recognize and receive revelations that reveal truth. If you discovered that a friend or someone you loved lied to you, how would you respond? You may respond with anger and the desire to strike back or get even.

Now, imagine having emptied yourself and looking at this experience with an open mind and heart, applying rational thought. Would your reaction be different? Would you receive a revelation about that person, about yourself or about your own life?

How about looking at a beggar who is asking you for money. You have your own financial challenges, and you work constantly just to get by. How do you react to the beggar? Do you see him as someone who refuses to take on responsibility and is just another leech introducing himself into your life?

Now empty your mind of all preconceived ideas and prejudices and approach the situation with an open mind, open heart, and rational thought. How do you now see the beggar? Is there a revelation you realized? We may learn a truth about ourselves, the real struggles of others, our inter-connectedness or how difficult it is for one to beg.

These revelations will reveal a truth about others, the world we live in or ourselves. Sometimes we dismiss these truths because they are too difficult to accept. A revelation may challenge us to look at another person or a group of people in a whole new way. It's painful to change directions and change the way we view things. The truth revealed to us may challenge us to look at ourselves and come to terms with our faults and frailties. This too can be difficult. They may jolt us, challenging us to look at the world in a whole new way. This can be painful.

We mentioned the big revelations like the beatitudes and the four noble truths. Consider how difficult it was for people to accept these truths. In modern history we see how much difficulty people had accepting freedom of the slaves, integration of the races, giving women the right to vote or equality of all. For many, these truths smacked at the heart of what they believed, and consequently led to the death of many messengers.

Many believe that they have arrived at truth when they simply follow the lead of society, getting the approval of others, especially from loved ones. They believe they have arrived at truth even when it defies anything rational or logical. In our pursuit of truth, we have to take the high ground and, as we previously mentioned, this will involve pain and suffering.

We cannot just "go along with" anymore. We have to remain open to receiving truths and then analyzing and embracing these revelations with our heart and mind, using both spiritual and rational faculties. Without reason we will not be able to recognize the truth they reveal. They will fail to do what they should be doing, shacking us out of our present reality and serving as the catalyst to embrace a new way of looking at things.

These truths should be jolting us, revealing not only that which is true externally, but the truth of our true nature. They should be teaching us who we truly are as human beings. They should be revealing to us our true nature; that which is at our Core.

It's impossible to be perfect or to create a perfect society, but we can move in that direction and get close to it if we are willing to receive and choose truth. We have to educate ourselves and use our intellect and reason for the sake of truth.

As difficult as it is, finding truth demands that we put aside the selfish appetites of mind and body. These appetites are important and also play a role in our journey, but they become a hindrance when they become our masters. We have an uncanny ability to warp truth in ways that suit our own pleasures, fears, or ego.

We are willing to go to great lengths to avoid the truth for the sake of comfort, power, possessions, pleasure or just maintaining the comforts we have found in the life we live. We have become so good at it that society requires courts and juries to try and sort out the facts and arrive at the truth.

We will all go through suffering in one way or another. Some go through divorce, and it often leads to anger, resentment, and bitterness.

How often does one view this experience as a revelation, revealing a truth about oneself? It can teach us much about ourselves by asking, with a clear mind and a willingness to face truth, "What went wrong? In what ways can I be a better person? What are my responsibilities from this experience? What kind of person am I at my core?"

Surely, no matter the circumstances around a divorce, no matter who was at fault, we can use this experience as a revelation that delivers a truth about life or ourselves. Being open to the revelation, willing to receive it and having it lead us to seeing and understanding our innermost nature. This will transform us and lead us to the state of happiness.

I was always amazed and inspired by many of the teens I counselled over the years. You would think that they would be too immature or lack the faculty of reason to receive revelations and accept the truths they impart. With many of them, this was not the case; perhaps because they had not been around long enough to have been completely manipulated by the media and a consumer society; perhaps because they had not yet subjected themselves to what society considers the status quo; or, it may have been because they had not yet bowed to a master, such as materialism, power, or ego. Consequently, they were innocent and open.

I found it quite profound how many of these teens react to family divorce, financial hardships and even experiences as gross as abuse and incest. I found them completely open to the truth; open to seeing that these events were not their fault; open to the truth that they are people of great talent with much to offer the world, in spite of the childhood they endured. They were open to accepting the truth that they are loved by friends, family, school community and God; in spite of having been given messages during their early years that they were un-loveable. They were able to see themselves as a person of love, with great potential to influence the world in a beautiful way.

In many cases, the youth would reveal profound truths to me that they came to realize through their hard life. They could see that in spite of everything, they were worthy of receiving love and capable of giving love. They could clearly see that they were called to be people of love. Some would clearly see their suffering as an opportunity to make something of their lives.

Street kids would often use their experiences as a guide to how not to live or be a parent. Many youth, from privileged backgrounds, would recognize that in spite of their wealth, there was a cancer in the home, that cancer being materialism. As an example, I had one young girl, who came from a wealthy but unhealthy family, say to me; "When you look at my house it appears to be beautiful, with its salacious size and expensive furniture, but really it is all a disguise for a cancer that grows within."

I often challenged myself after many of these sessions to become more like these youth: innocent children that could see truth better than I; to realize that I am being called to see clearly and receive truths. It is difficult and painful for us to receive and incorporate these revelations of truth.

We become trapped in the comforts or even the misery of the world we live in and refuse to accept truths that will make us uncomfortable. The challenge is to abandon our bias, empty ourselves of all that went before us, and receive these truths with an open mind and welcoming heart.

We are all being called to that which is true. We have been endowed with mind and the spirit to recognize and embrace it. We must be willing to reform our way of looking at things and the way in which we live our lives. We must love knowledge and truth above all else. When we make truth our pursuit, knowing our own limitations and strengths, we are moving in the direction of being a complete person. We are moving in the direction of becoming beings of love. We are moving inward and getting closer to our Core and finding happiness.

All of us have experienced at one time or another, the revelation of a truth that we recognize but choose to ignore.

Take for example the case of a couple in which one of them, or sometimes both of them, recognize that they are not meant for each other. They meet each other's needs in so many areas, but deep down they know they are not compatible. They feel it and see it, but they choose to ignore it. They do not allow these revelations to change the path of their life. A greater desire to be married, or being in love with the concept of family, or pressure from others, pushes them to make the decision to stay together.

How about the woman who sees small but significant signs of her partner's abuse or cheapness, and shrugs it aside for the sake of being in a relationship? How about the man who knows deep down that the woman he is with,

43

could never be a true friend and companion, and yet for the sake of lust, he fails to face the situation and end the relationship? Courage! It takes the ability to accept the revelation as truth and have the courage to change directions.

I have met many smart, hard-working people who refuse to give up on a business idea. Their ego and pride get in the way of seeing that the projects on which they have spent years, just won't work. Instead of using their gifted minds, strong work ethic and personal talents to move on to something new, they can't let go. Unfortunately, failure, heartache and bankruptcy become their destiny. Similarly, it's amazing how people with very high intelligence, fall into the pattern of making money or career their master, and fail to see how the very thing they thought would bring them happiness actually brings them misery.

In one of my past positions as a counsellor, a colleague spoke to me about her marriage. She expressed her frustrations with her husband not being romantic or exciting enough, and she wanted to leave him to explore other opportunities. I asked her a series of questions such as, "Does he treat you with respect? Is he a hard worker? Is he generous? Does he tell you he loves you? Is he a good father? Does he buy you gifts and take you out? Does he listen when you want to talk?"

To all these questions and others, she answered with a resounding "Yes!" Because she was thinking of leaving him we discussed the single life. In that discussion it was made evident that the single life has its fair share of disappointment and heartache. I asked her; "What if you met a man that gave you the excitement and romance you wanted but was missing most of those other things your husband gives you? Would you be willing to make the trade?" She was silent and left my office reflecting on what we discussed. I hope I had asked the right question.

We make every attempt to pursue the truth. To be willing to move away from that which is comfortable or may appear to be thrilling and in the direction of that which is true.

In many respects, truths are objective and universal.

They apply to all people in all times. For example: we are called to love and be a person for others; the earth circles the sun; the apple will fall from the tree because of gravity; drugs will destroy cells and eventually, one's health. These are universal truths.

However, what we do with such truths is up to each individual. To accept truths in a way that is best for that person's pursuit of true happiness, is up to them. Although the apple may fall on my head when I sit under the tree, I choose to sit under the tree because if the apple hits me in the head, it may awaken me, or I am willing to take the chance sitting under a tree and being hit by an apple because it is under that tree that I am able to meditate and see life more clearly.

The revelations we receive, combined with reason and an informed mind, will allow for truth to flourish. We will *be* truth. It will be in union with the divine within.

As humans, we cannot know absolute or perfect truth, but we can come to experience complete truth. Each revelation, learned through our experiences, will unveil a new treasure. These truths, on many levels and in many forms, all lead to the ultimate truth, that deep within we are beings of love.

You have heard it said that "ignorance is bliss." I disagree. If we ignore truth and see things only the way we want to see them, then truth is not that important. Some believe that this approach is actually a healthier one than seeing things the way they truly are. They think this way because this ignorant approach allows one to escape the suffering that comes with truth.

I would argue that true happiness is not possible when we ignore truth. If we are so attached to happiness that we ignore that which is true, true happiness escapes us. We may be giddy, smiling and laughing all the time, but when we ignore truth this is a false happiness. I call it slap happy.

Let's look at broken friendships. As tragic and devastating as broken friendships can be, they can also be a wonderful opportunity for renewal and transformation. If we are willing to embrace the suffering that comes with the experience of broken relationships, we will see truth and receive the enlightening experiences that accompany it. Many people react to a friendship that has ended with resentment, anger, and bitterness. They will find blame in every area and on every front in the other person. All of this is nonsense.

The truth of the matter is that none of us is perfect. We all make mistakes and it is not our mission to find fault; it is our mission to transform ourselves. This can be an opportunity to test our true character. We may be devastated and disappointed with the outcome, but do we wish *harm* or *happiness* for the other person? Will we try to destroy or make life better for the other person? This is a test of our character. This is a yardstick of our discovery of truth and our pilgrimage to happiness.

Happiness is impossible when we wish harm or are not kind-hearted or loving. Happiness is impossible if we do not clearly see the situation for what it truly is.

A colleague shared with me that years after his divorce he and his wife were still playing the blame game. The insults hurled at each other were as offensive and hurtful as they were during the divorce. I challenged him to look at life from her perspective. His wife had gone through a lot of suffering in her life, and the very foundation of her life had been rocked through many traumatic experiences. I pointed out to him that for some people, and perhaps in her case, projecting blame on another, or trying to impart guilt on another, is a result of misdirected anger or personal unresolved suffering due to tragedies.

During our discussion, I emphasized that his new mission was not to meet her insults with further insults, but rather to bring her comfort. Although they were no longer married, he nonetheless still has a duty to ease her suffering and help her on her path to happiness. What I am trying to point out here is that we have to make great effort to see the whole picture, to see and live truth.

While working with the Sisters of the Holy Trinity in Mexico I visited the place of their first monastery. It sat on a large piece of land which contained a beautiful structure. It took the Sisters almost a century to acquire the funds to build this structure for the girls who were either orphans, or were homeless. The corrupt Mexican government saw the value of this land and structure and took it from the Sisters. The corrupt military government provided them with another piece of land in a less desirable area. The Sisters went to work once again to build another orphanage and school for their girls.

As often as I tried to discuss this matter with them, they avoided any conversation that was resentful or bitter. They were accepting and forgiving, and more concerned with moving forward living a life of love. The truth was that resentment, bitterness, anger, or hatred would only impede them from loving and getting their job done.

I have often said that if I wanted to build a skyscraper I would need a thousand men; to build a city, a hundred Italians; to build a country, ten nuns. It is their ability to let go of the past that allows them to confront the future. They taught me that money does not matter; power does not matter; and competing for who is right does not matter. The only thing that matters is the task at hand. It is everything! This truth makes everything possible, especially living a fulfilled, purpose driven life.

If one is to seek true happiness, they must seek truth.

This driving force will allow one to discover things about self that are enlightening and transforming. What is it about self that caused one to choose this partner? What is it about self that created one's understanding of what love is? How do I communicate? In what ways do I demonstrate or fail to demonstrate my love? Do I truly know what love is?

There are so many questions to answer and so much reflection to do to find the truth and in so doing, understand self and become a better person. These kinds of questions, and the determination to move forward, is another step towards happiness. Like the Sisters, we cannot get entangled in the failures or the injustices. We cannot allow ourselves to become bitter and angry because of what has happened. If we do, we are never free from the prison we have built. We must be open to receiving the revelations and the truth they impart. We must pursue that person we truly are, and that person is a person of truth.

As we discussed, lifelong friendships sometimes end in a bitter break. As tragic as these experiences are, and as much suffering they bring, we must use them to ask the hard questions about self, and we must find the truth. There is no question that there are times when one person is not at fault, but even in these cases we can ask ourselves: Why it is that we would befriend such a person in the first place? How did we empower someone to behave the way they did? Why did we continue to foster an unhealthy relationship? The point here is we do not look to the other person's faults, but look within to discover what is true about ourselves.

Many suffer bad relationships with their boss or employer. There is no denying that there are many bosses who
are unfair, unjust, mad with power and arguably, somewhat crazy. The way your boss treats you, or your dismissal, may be completely unjustified and cruel. It is for the courts to determine justice in these cases.

However, in terms of your own search for truth, these injustices are opportunities for you to search deep within and discover wonderful things about yourself. Some use it as an opportunity to do an inventory of their life and their gifts.

They realize that in spite of this firing, but also because of this firing, they are much more gifted than they ever imagined. They may discover that this job was not right for them; or on a more spiritual level, they come to understand their own tolerance and acceptance of the mental illness or sins of another. Their ability for forgiveness and mercy is tested.

In all these cases, there are wonderful opportunities to see and accept new truths about the world and ourselves.

We recognize that if we become preoccupied with judging the other, hurling insults at them, creating slanderous and hateful talk about them, we will be blind to what is true. In all things we must remain kind-hearted, even toward our oppressor. This does not mean that we love falsely, or do not use courts and other bodies to seek justice. We remain kind-hearted in the sense that we do not wish any evil on them, and do not waste time and energy with bitterness, resentment, and hatred. Instead, we choose to accept that which is true, that which we were created to be and in that search we will discover that forgiveness, love, and kind-heartedness is the answer to continuing the path to happiness.

As previously mentioned, revelations will come to us in big and small ways. Once again, while working with the Sister of Holy Trinity in Mexico, there was an evening I found particularly fascinating. As I sat and talked with a number of the Sisters, I observed off in the distance, at the end of the room, an older Sister working with one of the younger girls. The older Sister worked for two hours with the younger girl unraveling a tangled ball of thread. Thread was important in the mission because sewing was taught as one of the trades. In order for the thread to be used, it had to be unraveled and re-raveled.

What I found frustrating was entertaining for the sister and young girl. They laughed and relished the task. Occasionally they would look up at me and the other Sisters and give us a smile. I was tempted to grab the ball of thread, throw it out the window and shout, "Don't worry about it, I will buy you a hundred of those!" Instead, I watched, and this experience turned out to be a wonderful revelation. It taught me about patience, the value of the smallest of things, and the unique and wonderful ways in which bonding between young and old can occur.

These revelations that impart truth will come in many shapes and sizes, big and small. They will come at different times, anticipated and unexpected. They will come in many forms, jolting, and calming.

What is important is that you are ready to receive them. You won't discard them as an inconvenience. You will not dismiss them as unimportant or irrelevant. It is a life-long process; truths being revealed to you until the day you die. You will be open and alert, free of self and surrendering to these truths that life offers.

The Dalai Lama states that a peaceful or meditative mind comes from a warm-heartedness. If we can reduce ill feelings toward another, we will reduce distrust. This in itself is a truth and doing this opens us up to receiving the beautiful truths others have to offer. We have to remain focused on the good in life so that we will become more trusting and able to surrender to the wonderful revelations. Anger, hatred, jealousy, arrogance, and an obsessive desire do not leave us in a state of mind that is conducive to receiving truths.

You could be washing the floor in your home or cooking a meal for your family and suddenly there is a mini explosion in your mind, revealing to you the profound truth regarding the importance of the work you are doing. You may see that this simple act is a great act of love and realize the intimate interconnectedness of your family. You could be walking in a park, having a conversation with a stranger, working on the job, or attending a funeral and receive a wonderful revelation that introduces a truth into your life.

While I was working in the mountains of the Dominican with the poorest of people, they told me that they would pray for me. "Pray for me," I thought. "Why would *they* pray for *me*?" Upon reflection, this one statement brought me to a wonderful revelation and truth. I realized that *I was in need of prayers*. In spite of my economic comforts, opportunities, health, and career, I was in need of their prayers. I also realized that although I went there to help them at their disadvantage, they actually had more to offer me than I had to offer them.

I visited Rwanda ten years after the genocide that took the life of over 800,000 people, mostly Tutsi. While working in the village of Musha, mostly occupied by Tutsi, I asked them how they could live side by side with the Hutu. Some of these Hutu and their family members were involved in the slaughter of the Tutsi ten years prior. They simply responded, "We are all Rwandans now, we are all brothers and sisters." I received a powerful truth.

The key ingredient to end war, to live in community and to prosper is measured by our capacity to forgive. This

51

experience also served as an internal catalyst forcing me to ask, "do I truly forgive, or do I just talk and lecture on forgiveness?"

This revelation was then followed by a story they shared with me. When the Hutu military came to kill all the Tutsi in a village and surrounding farms, one of the Tutsi families hid in the field. They hid in the ground, underneath the straw and dirt where the goats grazed. When the Hutu came and did not see anyone, they asked a neighbour where the family had run. To save her own life she told them that they were hiding in the ground. The soldiers went over and killed all of them—adults and children, except for one.

The mother of the children was hiding in an area where the goats were grazing. The soldiers neglected this part of the land. The genocide ended and a couple of years passed. One of the missionaries was driving his jeep into the city with some of the villagers to get food and supplies. One of those in the jeep was the mother who had hidden where the goats were grazing.

The missionary and the others spotted the woman who told soldiers about the family that was hiding. The mother asked the missionary to stop the jeep. She got out, went over to the woman, placed her arms around her and told her that she forgave her. This supernatural ability to forgive is an example which reveals a truth and gives us a peek through the window into the Divine.

By placing ourselves in the right state of mind, heart, and spirit, we will embrace these truths revealed to us. No matter how painful the truth is, we will admit that our previous way of looking at things was wrong. These truths will serve as catalysts, propelling us to seek Truth. They inspire us to continue to empty ourselves to receive more truths.

The closer we go to the Core, we come to recognize more and more that these truths reveal to us that at our Core, we are beings of love. We are called to love because that is what we are.

Consequently, to find true happiness we must be a people of love. This is the ultimate truth that we discover.

Here are some questions that may assist you on your journey to recognize, embrace and be transformed by your revelations:

1. What revelations have I received over the past week that I would have normally dismissed?

2. What truths did these revelations reveal to me about myself and the world?

3. In what ways have I found it uncomfortable, challenging and even painful to accept these revelations?

REALIZATION

"Radiate boundless love towards the entire world."– The Buddha

My second promise: "I promise to live this new me, founded on truth, and become the person of love that truth calls me to be."

We can be encouraged by the words of the Dalai Lama: "The practice of compassion gives me the greatest satisfaction. Whatever the circumstances, whatever the tragedy I am faced with, I practice compassion. That reinforces my inner strength and brings me happiness, by giving me the feeling that my life is useful."

You have completed step one, Reception. This step required you to put yourself in the right state of heart and mind, and receiving truth. These truths you have received have brought you to step two, *realizing many truths*, with the ultimate truth being that at our Core we are beings of love.

To be truly happy by being who we are, we must become a person for others. Being this person of love means shaking off clinging, confusion, neediness, fear and grasping to self, shaking off all the entanglements, attachments, prejudices, distractions, and opinions that have enslaved you. You have become just one thing, a person of love.

Jesus, the Buddha, and other religious leaders have been clear on this; we are called to live a life of love. It's a wonderful realization! It's not pleasure, material things or a life free of suffering that we long for; it is a life of love. It can involve inconvenience, sacrifice and even suffering, nevertheless, it is living the life of love we are called to live.

It is pure love that is at the Core. Love is what we truly are. It is what it means to be fully human. Consequently, it is what brings happiness.

Love is at the root of our existence. The need for affection is in our DNA. Many studies have demonstrated this reality.

Studies have shown that infant development, brain development and the child's happiness hinges on the affection and compassion they receive. The need for affection is at the root of our existence. We are interdependent in this way. Compassion is our true nature. It brings happiness to self and others. Being a loving being is not just the ability to love all that is outside of yourself, it also means you are able to accept love from others.

You are also open to letting love in.

In spite of love and compassion being that which conquers all that ails us, it is often viewed as naïve and embarrassing to express. Those who fall to this view that love is embarrassing and a weakness, end up fearful, anxious, disorientated and suffer the worst of all human experiences, loneliness. Giving love and receiving love should not be embarrassing. In fact, we should not hesitate to be expressive with our love. We shouldn't be afraid to hug people, to shake the hand of a stranger, to touch a beggar and to stare into the eyes of another with a look of gentleness and caring.

Love is infinite. Rather than being an energy that is directed toward a person or thing, it can roam infinitely, not directed toward anything. It is boundless and just is what we are. To love only when the conditions are optimal for love or only when it brings a return is not real love. Loving is more than just an action directed toward something; it is an energy that has no direction...it just is. It can occupy all and every aspect of our life.

We don't have to calculate how to love in a particular situation...we already love. This is pure love; the love we find at the center of our being.

I hope you are not disappointed. Perhaps you thought that these truths would reveal to you something different. Perhaps you thought they would reveal information about economics, how to be prosperous, or something scientific.

Truths will reveal many things to you, in all areas of life, but the one true realization is that we are beings of love, called to love and to be a person for others.

This love is the stuff of life. It is the essence of life. Everything that we now think or do, in our personal life or career, is shaped by this being of love we have become. Being a person of love will enrich every aspect of our lives: relationships, career, and friendships.

Fr. Hermann Schulz, a Salesian Catholic priest, was sent to Rwanda to help some of the poorest people in the world. As a young boy of five years old, Father Hermann had lost his father. He witnessed his father getting shot as they darted across a field to escape bombs and heavy fire during the Second World War.

Young Hermann and his mother became refugees and lived a life of poverty, forced to beg for many years. He decided as a young boy that when he grew up he would do all he could to prevent any child from experiencing hunger. Consequently, he became a priest and asked to be sent to the poorest country in the world.

He dedicated his life to loving the poor children of Rwanda. He became what he was created to be...a person of love. In being this person for others, he found happiness.

When the Salesian Fathers sent him to Rwanda, he had no idea of the degree of poverty and the harsh life he would experience. He suffered constant bouts of malaria, confronted corruption in the government and military, faced extreme poverty and witnessed many horrible sights. His life was threatened on numerous occasions.

When I asked him why he never left, he answered, "I told the children I loved them. How do you leave someone after you tell them you love them?" Not to undermine the profound words of Father Hermann, I believe his reason for staying is much deeper than a love directed toward these children. It is because he has become and is a person of love. If he had never been introduced to Rwanda, his love would still be as boundless as it is. It would find another recipient, although being a person of love does not mean that your love needs to find a receiver. Love is what you are, and that energy source finds its way into an endless number of subjects.

The missionaries' unconditional love for all demonstrates that love is for more than families, friends, and colleagues. It is for all people, without discrimination. It is directed toward the universe and all its parts, even our enemies. There are no boundaries or lines to be drawn. Hence, it creates internally a sense of calm and inter-connectedness. Externally, it creates a world of peace and harmony.

Father Hermann's revelation came to him as a young boy, and he was receptive to the truths that came with it. The truth revealed to him was that there is great suffering in the world, and we are called, in spite of injustice and oppression, to be a person for others. He could have easily chosen to be bitter and angry, or he could have chosen to make money his master, becoming prosperous enough that poverty would never threaten him again. Because he was open to receiving the truth he chose love.

There are many stories like Father Hermann's. We all know of people who have had a terrible or tragic experience and from those experiences, they realized that love was the answer. They realized that true happiness and living a full and fruitful life, comes from living a life of love. I'm sure that you can think of many great people throughout history that endured great injustice and suffering and yet, they chose to be a person for others. These are the Gandhi's and the Mother Theresa's of the world.

In our own lives or through the lives of people we know, we have witnessed the tragedy of abandonment, divorce, bankruptcy, sickness, and death. For some, these experiences serve as a revelation bringing them to the realization that happiness is found in responding with love, and living a life of love. Through these experiences they were brought to their knees, thus allowing them to be stripped of all they were, and forging in them a new person. Others become angry, bitter, mistrusting, and unable to love again. They imprison themselves in a world of darkness.

Ask yourself, "How do I receive my experiences and revelations in life? Do I choose to see them as the revelations that they are, pointing me to truth? Do I see the ultimate truth being that I, at my Core, am a being of love? Am I at that mental and spiritual place where I realize that I am called to be a loving person for others, healing them and bringing them to higher ground?"

If we want to be happy, we must choose love. If we want our life to be full and fruitful, we must choose love. If we want to be content and at peace, we must choose love. If we want to live a life with meaning and purpose, it must be a life of love. Living a life of love brings true happiness because it is what we are, beings of love. It is love that is at the human Core, the Christ nature, the Bodhi nature. Happiness is impossible without being a person of love because without love, we are not being our true self.

While working at the House of Malnutrition and Dying in Haiti, I held an infant dying of starvation. It was a gruesome sight holding this skeleton in my arms and looking at her hanging skin and bulging eyes. As I tried to comfort her and meet her suffering with gentle smiles I saw in her face, the face of my daughter. At that moment I realized that this is my daughter, that we are all brothers and sisters in one family.

The revelation was traumatic, bringing me to the stark realization that this child was my child, and her suffering was my suffering. It was tempting to dismiss the revelation and return to the mission, comfortable in the thought that I did good deeds that day, and those good deeds are enough. It is much more difficult to accept that we are all one family, brothers, and sisters and that my love is infinite, without limits, conditions, or boundaries.

Being a person of love involves a change in our attitudes and our actions. It involves a change in our being. This new way of life may be contrary to the way many others live, and you may feel out of place, but your greatness will be respected and admired. You may feel out of place, because judging others is commonplace, and you no longer judge. Father Hermann did not judge the military that killed his father, nor those who left him and his mother to a life of poverty. He never judged the government in Rwanda, even though he was subjected to injustice and threats. He never judged hunger and human suffering, or why God would allow such a thing. He only witnessed it and responded.

He responded not by asking 'why,' rather he responded with 'what.' He chose to take his suffering and forge a shovel rather than a sword, to re-build a broken world and heal others. He chose to love, and this reaction to his revelations created a better and safer world for thousands of young children, and brought him happiness.

I had the honour to talk with a Buddhist monk of the Theravada sect. He lives a strict monastic life and follows the Eightfold Path to achieve Enlightenment. I asked him if anyone in the monastery, including the Master, had achieved Enlightenment. He was quick to respond that they do not make that judgment of themselves or each other. He told me that there is no reason to make such a judgment because it serves no purpose. Nothing would be accomplished by such a judgment. In fact, it may hinder their journey to greater levels of Enlightenment. He lived in a world of love, absent of judging.

Similarly, the Sisters of the Holy Trinity in Mexico never found need or time to judge. In spite of being repeatedly robbed by thieves, taken advantage of by the government and the local people, they would never judge. Their single solitary concern was their work. They always focused on loving. The question they asked themselves every day was, "What do I need to accomplish today?" They chose only love.

Love means living a life free of judging. The drug addiction is our addiction, the gambler's addiction is our addiction, the mental illness of another is our mental illness, and the poverty of another is our poverty. All that concerns us is loving. We are one with our inner Core, one with the Christ-like nature. Consequently, we are beings of love, and in living this life we find happiness.

Michael is the founder of three orphanages in Haiti. While working there I met a young man who had betrayed him. While Michael was visiting the US to raise more money for his orphanages, one of the boys he raised in his orphanage, now a young man, turned against Michael stealing money and getting donors to send money to him. This betrayal was so devastating that it almost resulted in the closing of the orphanages. When Michael returned, the man who betrayed him was banished and Michael spent months trying to repair and recover from the theft and betrayal. The young man eventually returned to the orphanage and begged Michael for forgiveness. Michael forgave him and accepted him back into the organization.

Sometime later Michael made him the director of one of the orphanages. It was actually the most difficult orphanage, a home for the severely disabled children left on the streets. He served as a stellar leader, caring for these children like few could. Michael, being a man of great love, a love directed towards all people, even his enemies, had the capacity to forgive and show mercy. In the end, love proved to be the answer.

When you read the life and teachings of the great spiritual leaders, you quickly recognize that the two greatest sins are the sins of pride and self-righteousness. People who are truly liberated and one with the Christ-like nature, never view themselves as "better than" or having accomplished "more than." They only facilitate the work of others. They see themselves as humble servants. They are *completely wrapped up in loving.* Their focus is not to accuse the sinner, but to love the sinner.

With love there is no one who is better than or less than. There is only the "other" who is "me." There is only love. Be patient! Be patient with yourself and the world. Be patient with the loving you have chosen to do. Love demands patience.

No doubt, as we previously discussed, abandoning much of what you were, through this journey to your Core, will bring you suffering. It is not easy to be different than most, but most are not happy. It is not easy to empty yourself and let go, but for the sake of your own happiness you must. "For those who want to save their life will lose it, and those who lose their life for my sake will find it" (Matthew 16:24). This new way of living, being a person for others, will involve sacrifice and suffering. However, paradoxically, it is the life that will bring you happiness.

Many years ago I went through bankruptcy, divorce and the death of a loved one, all in a short period of time. I was going through great suffering. In spite of going to priests, counselors, and psychologists, I continued to spiral downward. It was two sentences said to me by my father that changed my life in an instant.

My father asked me, "Do you believe that someday your children will also go through suffering?"

"Of course," I answered.

"And from whom will they have learned how to suffer?" replied to my father.

At that moment I was jolted into a different reality. I was able to rise above self-pity and myself and think of my children.

With just a few words, I changed my way of thinking and began to heal. While I and everyone else had dwelt on my misfortune and suffering, my father challenged me to rise above myself and think of others. In so doing, he challenged me to be a person for others. In this case, a person for my children. I continued to suffer but my suffering was different, and the healing began.

You are no longer at war with yourself or the world. You are free! Free to love. Free from preconceived ideas and prejudices, free from jealousy, judging, anger, bitterness, resentment, and regret. You are free from your "self." No matter your profession in life, you are free to use the greatness within, the divine that resides at your Core, to be an instrument of love, a healing agent in a broken world. You can now take your specific gifts and talents and use them in living out this new mission of loving, this oneness with the Divine within and subsequent oneness with the world. To approach all of life with love, is *happiness*.

It goes without saying how wonderful we feel when we express our affection to family and friends. What better feeling is there than when you show love to your children or spouse or brothers and sisters. What better feeling when we have an open heart to accept their love.

You will be completely fulfilled in your new life as a healer and elevator of others. You will live a life of healing, and you will cherish your mission to elevate others through all that you do and all that you are. A simple smile, a kind word, a helping hand, a gentle voice, playing the role of peacemaker, devotion to your family and friends, working in the Third World, being a doctor, being a mechanic...no matter what you do, you do it in love and for the purpose, in a small or big way, to heal another.

Fr. Lou Quinn, in the Dominican, built hundreds of homes for the poor. He would go from village to village transforming the way they live. When I visited these communities, I was amazed to discover how they chose who the next house would be built for. Father had his own method of choosing which families would get a home and the order in which they were built.

At times, he broke the mold of his own system to accommodate what the people wanted. Often, the next person in line would forfeit their position if they believed that someone else in the community was in greater need than they were. This is love. Consider what this kind of love does, in building community. It certainly is a measure of greatness, actualizing the philosophy, "How great a nation we will be determined by how we treat our weakest members."

As we live this new way of life, we must continue to meditate or pray. Prayer not only reminds us of the revelations, our transformation and enlightenment, it *sustains* the level of this new way of living. Prayer does not allow us to forget the revelation or to move away from it. There is temptation even in happiness. We will be tempted to fall back into old ways.

Amazingly, as happy as we are, we will be tempted to fall back into unhappiness.

This is part of our human frailty and weakness, just as it is for the addict who gives up the drugs, has never felt better, returns to the life of drugs. Prayer and meditation will give us the strength and clarity to remain on the track of happiness; living a life that seeks truth and lives love. One form of such meditation would be to continually repeat to yourself the promises you have made.

A weightlifter must continue with frequent training. As soon as the training becomes less frequent, the lifter begins to lose strength and size. A runner must continue to run. If the running stops, the runner quickly loses cardiovascular conditioning.

Similarly, for an individual and for a community, prayer is essential to remain at those heights of healer and elevator. An alcoholic will tell you that regular attendance at meetings is essential to sobriety. A religious community will tell you that regular communal prayer is critical to the life, breath, and success of a community. A celibate priest, nun or Buddhist monk will tell you that daily prayer/meditation is necessary to retain their level of spirituality and enlightenment. Choose the path of strengthening that is best for you. Certainly, you have to recite the promises you have made every day, and throughout the day.

Some measure of prayer, meditation or reciting the promises will help you resist the temptation to fall back into old ways. For the sake of true happiness, we will be tempted by momentary happiness. Acting morally in perfect harmony and balance with the universe will, at times, be very difficult. We have to remind ourselves that we are called to be love! Societal view of success, our own desires and passions, and our need to be part of the herd are strong temptations that can easily pull up away from the true happiness we presently live. Amazingly, we can fall back and choose present and false happiness over true and everlasting happiness.

The temptation to retreat back always exists. The lives of great prophets, spiritual leaders, and saints is evidence of the temptation to slip back. Even when these revelations and realizations are profound, we will always be tempted to retreat, to choose that which is easy, comfortable, and routine. Our revelations and realizations of what is true will also move us in ways that challenge public opinion. We will face obstacles as we proclaim and live this truth. It may result in us being ridiculed and isolated. "Hold on to what is true, what is honourable, what is just and what is pure." (Phil.4:8). There will always be attempts to knock us off the path. Society's way is not the way to the Core.

We can persevere in our knowledge that we are on the path to complete happiness. As travelers on this pilgrimage, we must live a life of prayer/meditation to sustain the openness to accepting new revelations, adopting truth, and living love.

In Mexico, we would go out every day to meet the street kids. It was understood that there was always an open invitation for them to enter the mission. Many of them, however, were so addicted to drugs, the street life and/or prostitution, that it was a difficult decision for them to make.

The Sisters would not pressure them to enter the mission. Instead, the Sisters would go out every day to check on them, council them, educate them and offer them food. The kids were depleted emotionally, psychologically, and physically.

However, before they ate, the kids always insisted on praying. They would gather in a circle, put their arms around each other and pray. In the midst of their chaos and suffering, they saw it as important to pray together. It was what sustained them, keeping them in touch with the beauty in their ugly world. Prayer reminded them of their blessings, but the temptation of the streets was too great to resist.

No matter what we do in life, we make it holy by the love we bring to our work. One type of work is no more important than another. It is all about the love we infuse into work. Ask yourself whose work is more important: the person on Wall Street doing billion-dollar deals or the personal support worker who lovingly bathes and cares for the elderly.

No matter what we do, if we are motivated and guided by love, if we have become a being of love, then our work is a vocation that will bring us true happiness. It is not the work itself, but the love we bring to it, that brings us happiness. Our work merely becomes an extension of what we already are, a person of love. When being a person of love, all our work is transformed from a job to a vocation.

In our career and work, we will no longer see ourselves as above another. We will no longer be apart from the "other." We will "be with" the other. A doctor will "be with" and serve the patient when the doctor is equal with the patient. A counsellor will "be with" their client when the counsellor is equal with the client.

A friend will truly "be with" a friend when they are equal with the friend. We are equal with one another because their weakness is our weakness, their suffering is our suffering, their struggles are our struggles. We will see ourselves as we truly are—people who "are with" others—in communion with them as one human family, cultivating in each other a finding of happiness.

When we become beings of love, happiness is always found in the moment. We no longer dream of happiness in the future. We are happy in the present because it is not a better job, a better spouse, a better house that will bring happiness. It is all that we think and do that brings us happiness because we are beings of love and love brings happiness in the now.

We have given examples of love in this chapter. We have looked at the actions and life of missionaries who have become people of love, but we may still desire a clear definition of what this love is and what kind of life it leads us live. We have to realize that love transcends human language and any definition.

However, being human and people of rational thought, we demand such a definition. Even though we know that this person of love we become is beyond definition, here is an attempt at providing what it means for us:

We have shed all that we were and become something greater.

⦿ We are truly liberated, free from prejudices, anger, resentments, bitterness, and hatred.

⦿ We are free of ego, our past, fears, social pressures, and comforts.

⦿ We are non-judgmental, making us all one person, connected in a web of humanity.

⦿ We are unselfish and infinite, living a way of life that expects nothing in return.

⦿ We are calm, kind-hearted, righteous, and just.

⦿ Our words and actions transform and redeem us and others.

⦿ We don't just heal one thing; we heal all things.

◻ In our every thought and action, we are a person for others.

◻ Matthew 25:35-36: "For I was hungry, and you gave me something to eat, I was thirsty, and you gave me something to drink, I was a stranger and you invited me in, I needed clothes, and you clothed me, I was sick, and you looked after me, I was in prison, and you came to visit me."

◻ St. Paul in 1Cor. 4-7:, said, "Love is patient, love is kind. It does not boast; it is not proud. It does not dishonour others, it is not self-seeking, it is not easily angered, it keeps no record of wrongs. Love does not delight in evil but rejoices with the truth. It always protects, always trusts, always hopes, always preserves. Love never fails."

If we looked at the definition of love in other religions, we would find that it is similar if not identical to what we have outlined here. Buddhism describes love as loving kindness, compassion, appreciative joy, and equanimity (mental calmness).

I believe that, given the limitations of human language, living out the virtues is the best way to describe the new person we have become and the life we now live. The virtues describe not only the person we are internally, but the actions we express externally. They describe the new you in Motion.

As a summary to the first two ingredients of the formula for happiness, remember what Gandhi said: "When I despair, I remember that all through history the way of truth and love has always won."

The Following are some questions that may serve you in helping you become the person of love you are called to be:

1. In what ways is being a person of love different from the life I previously lived?

2. What are some of the challenges I will face, internally and externally, being this new person of love?

3. What kind of impact will I have on my friends, family, colleagues and myself, through being this person of love?

REFORMATION

"Being virtuous and doing good involves suffering but is worth it because it brings health and happiness to self and others." – P.T.

My third promise: "I promise to put this new me, a person of love and founded in truth, into motion through living out the eight key virtues."

The mere act of helping someone makes us feel better inside. Reaching out to help another, to heal a broken world in any capacity, makes us feel better about what we do, about the person we are, and about the world we create.

Even the simplest of acts can forge strong relationships, build communities, and bring together people from all over the world. It may not appear evident, but even the smallest of acts can produce a ripple effect reaching farther than we can imagine. These good relationships are based on love and keep us healthy and happy. As Mark Twain said, "There is only time for loving."

Upon reaching the Core, we have discovered and embraced the Divine, we can now live a life that goes beyond the five senses, the intellect, and emotions. Yet this life fully uses, to its maximum capacity, the five senses, the intellect, and the emotions. We now live a life empowered, experiencing the oneness of the universe. We are reformed and we put into motion the new person we have become, healing and elevating others.

This new you will experience awe and splendor as you live a life of serving others. You are no longer captive to those things that society has deemed necessary for a happy life. You no longer fear losing material possessions. You no longer seek praise for your actions. You are free of attachments. You no longer live in isolation. You are liberated from judging others and from living your life in accordance with what others deem is worthy.

You will continue to carry on with your regular life. You will live an ordinary life but live it in an extra-ordinary way. You now live life seeing and experiencing your Oneness with everything and everyone. You desire to create a better world through healing and elevating others. You live your life for others, going through your days with the single mission to heal others and elevate them to higher ground. Although you will remind yourself often of your promises and use different techniques and strategies to maintain your enlightenment, you will now find that this new life of loving becomes natural for you. It is so much a part of who you actually are, you will love before cognitively reminding yourself to love.

Your quest and knowledge of truth, your love and desire to heal others, coupled with the great resources within you will enable you to live a purpose-filled life. You will do great things, even with the smallest of things. You will continue with your same work, your same career, your same position in life, but it will be performed in a whole new way.

Power, status, prestige, and money are no longer your goals. Your goal, in all that you do in your work and personal life, is motivated by love. You are one with the Christ within, the Bodhi nature, the Tao.

Living this new life does not mean that we ignore our material needs or the needs of our family. It does not mean that we abandon our work or career for a life of asceticism. It does not mean we are foolish with financial and other resources, or allow others to take advantage of our new way of living. If we allow others to take advantage of us, we only feed the beasts within them. Rather than creating a world of true love and healing, this would perpetuate a world of greed and self satisfaction.

It is inevitable that this new way of living, seeing everyone, even our enemies, as our brothers and sisters, will certainly lead to others trying to take advantage of us, but we will see clearly that which is abusive or evil. We will recognize the wolf in sheep's clothing. We are not attached to ideologies, political systems and even our own emotions. We are free of these things that may present themselves as love, but are not.

They are not true love.

How can we, with language as a limited form of communication, describe this new way of life? How can we best describe our new attitudes and actions? Just as the concept of being a loving being transcends language, so does any explanation of this new life we live. Given this, the best explanation is to describe such a person as one who embodies the eight key virtues.

This new life, now put into motion, is best demonstrated by the person who lives the virtuous life. Living in union with our true nature, our Christ-like nature, is living a life expressed in the virtues.

Aristotle claimed that there are many factors that bring us happiness, but one cannot be happy without being virtuous: a good and noble person. The virtues give expression and form to the divine love, which we have come to realize as being the new us, and the source of our happiness. I would argue that virtues are universal and innate. We see this when we reach our Core.

They are objective truths that are self-evident. They best express the person we have become, and they are guiding principles in all that we do. They are in themselves a life in motion that promotes and actualizes peace, purpose, oneness, prosperity, and happiness. On a practical and more secular level, living the virtues will not only bring better health, but will result in you flourishing in your career and the everyday choices you make.

Before we look at the virtuous life, it is important to understand the concept of motion. I am reluctant to use the word action because this limits our understanding of being a person of love and living the life of love, to those who are physically healthy. Motion is lived out in many ways and forms, and no form is more or less important than another. For example, a sick or dying person, restricted to bed life, is able to put their love into motion through their communication with their nurse, through the way in which they accept their suffering, or through silent prayer for a broken world.

Too often, we associate the significance of one's life by the amount of action they exude, but this approach is incomplete and misguiding. The one who lays sick in bed and prays for the healing of a broken world is as important as the one who goes to work every day. The person in bed who is kind to their nurse and communicates their love and gratitude for them is as significant as the nurse who cares for the person's needs. Both are living a life in motion. Both are significant. All acts of kindness play a role in changing the world.

No matter your physical condition, your state of health, your economic situation or your position in life, you will be a person in motion, expressed through the virtues you live. And, by being this person in motion, even in a dire situation, you will experience happiness. There are eight virtues you now are, and now live.

The Eight Key Virtues

1. *Humility*

It is no wonder that many of the great leaders, thinkers and inventors were humble. Great people are not consumed by their vanity and because of this they can focus on that which is greater than self; living a life for the greater common good. This is not only the ethical life; it is the full and flourishing life.

Nobody wants to be around a "know it all." Spouses, children, employees, employers, friends, and family all avoid that person who "knows it all." People want to be around others who are open to learning new things, are attentive and good listeners and are grateful for the knowledge and experiences that are shared with them. People want to be around those who are humble. It is good to be humble. It is good for your marriage, your home life, your relationships, and your workplace. Humility is a key ingredient to being successful at everything you do.

I was amazed at the humility Father Lou Quinn exercised with his organization in the Dominican. As I mentioned, he started with one shovel, and his organization grew to include hundreds of workers and volunteers. They built roadways, schools, houses, irrigation systems, a hospital, a university and more. The list of his accomplishments is inspiring and staggering.

When I sat through a long meeting he had with his executives, Father Lou rarely spoke, and when he did, he spoke softly. Here is a man who was viewed by the Dominicans as a living saint, a giant in the world. Yet, if you were a stranger and sat in one of those meetings, you would hardly notice his presence. Humility is a powerful virtue in motion, inspiring others, empowering others, and laying the foundation for them to do great things.

Adopting humility is one of the greatest freedoms we can experience. Imagine how wonderful it is to never have to boast, prove yourself, or be wrapped up with yourself. Think of how freeing it is, to empty yourself of ego and to approach every new situation like a child, eager and hungry to learn; to receive new and exciting truths and have them shape you into greatness.

Some view humility as a weakness. They would prefer to convince others that they already possess the truths and know best. Their life involves being manipulative, desperate to always be in control of others. How miserable life must be for the spouse who tries to impose their will on their partner, or the parent who imposes their will on their child. Are you an employee who has a manager that imposes their will on you? Have you given thought of how miserable their life must be?

These people are prisoners, enslaved in their own self-righteousness, closed-minded to everything new and wonderful. They travel through life, expending a lot of wasted energy, creating a master-slave relationship, and denying human freedom. Conformity and obedience become their benchmark of excellence. There is no spirit of openness, or any chance to receive revelations and be transformed. There is no room for greatness or the latitude to do truly good works.

To be without humility is destructive on the personal as well as corporate level. It is not good for the individual, the relationship, the community, or the organization. Pride, arrogance, and self-righteousness are the opposites of humility and are not characteristic of a life in motion. It is a stagnant life because this person believes they possess all they need. There is no reason to reach out, to explore or to move forward. They believe they have already arrived.

When I ask Father Lou Quinn how he started, he simply

answered, "With a shovel. I picked up a shovel and started digging my way up the mountain." He recognized that roads were needed, so that the people could be with one another, accessing and sharing the necessities of life. As he took up his shovel and started to dig, so did others. Before long, all people of the village were digging with him. He began simply with humility. He didn't bring in bulldozers or a crew of paid workers.

This single humble act mobilized the entire village, and eventually an entire province in the Dominican. It was not long before roads, schools, hospitals, and an entire economy was created. This is what we are called to: humble acts of love.

And we find comfort in the words of Mahatma Gandhi who said,

"When you are fighting in a just cause, people seem to rise right out of the pavement to help you, even when it is dangerous."

Humility is a powerful virtue in motion.

Humility is a sign of profound courage, living a life that surrenders to all the beauty that life has to offer. It is courage because it means taking the risk to be like a child, who looks at the world with open eyes, eager to absorb all that it offers.

Think of how wonderful and exciting your life is now with every conversation filled with questions of intrigue and curiosity. Think of how great we can be if we remain humble, wanting to relish and grow from each new revelation, always in a state of receiving truths! You will exemplify curiosity, approaching every situation with the innocence of a child, eager to learn and inspired by the wonder of things, and the fruit of your curiosity will be insight and intuition.

With humility, you are able to accept your weaknesses and admit to your ignorance. This is a characteristic of wisdom. It will allow you to fall to your knees in recognizing and accepting that which is true. It will prevent you from being proud and self-righteous, distant, and isolated from others.

Your life will be in motion, absorbing all it has to offer and living a life for others. Humility is an active virtue, affecting every part of your life and the lives of those around you. You approach life and people with zeal and enthusiasm, eager to learn, love and to serve others. People will find you wise, hospitable, caring, and they will be eager to be around you. People will be inspired by you and through your humility you will empower them to be great. Your humility will elevate others, challenging them to believe in themselves, take the reins and change the world.

2.Gratitude

During my work in the deplorable slums of Haiti, I met a young boy who resided there. He spoke of his hard life. He said that although he lives in misery, he chooses not to be miserable.

He thanked God every day for three things. First, the gift of breath, for he is alive another day. Secondly, for the gift of his legs, so he can run to find food or work. Thirdly, for the gift of his mind, so he can dream of a better day. A grateful mind allows us to receive revelations and inspirations, to view every day as a blessing and like this young boy, to move forward. A grateful mind fills every day, no matter our situation, with cheerfulness.

When we are not grateful, we are consumed with attaining more things, in hopes of being satisfied. An ungrateful mind is negative and often too bitter to receive new and wonderful revelations. But you now live with a grateful mind, continuing to receive revelations, being inspired, and approaching every situation with a joy. This is a state of mind, a way of living, rather than just moments in your life.

In Medjugorje, parents with babies held in their arms make the long pilgrimage on their knees to the Basilica. It's terribly painful. I found it hard to watch. They make a pilgrimage of gratitude for the gifts God gave them. They may be poor and living a harsh life, but they are grateful. A man I observed doing this with his child in his arms had gratitude for the gift of the child he carried.

You will no longer be a person who finds gratitude only after you have lost something. You will be grateful for all of it, the joy, and the suffering. You will be in that state of mind that allows you to move forward, regardless of what life hands you.

You will be the person who can live in misery, without being miserable. No matter the present situation, you live a life of gratitude in the now! There is no yesterday or tomorrow for the grateful person, there is only now. People will want to be around you because you are happy and content, seeing the good in all things, even suffering. They will be inspired by you. You will be a positive influence on their lives.

The new life becomes one of gratitude, wherein we embrace the defeats, sorrows, sufferings, and failures. You are grateful because they are experiences that bring with them a continuing emptying of self, a oneness with humanity, and a humility to begin anew.

When you are grateful for all things, you approach and live life in a completely different way. You approach life with your heart always open. When you reach out to serve others, and when your acts of love appear to make no difference, you are grateful that you were able to serve. When you help someone and they do not show any appreciation, you are not deterred. Your gratitude is not conditional or measured by results. It is just there. It just exists in all you think, do and are.

Consequently, it brings with it purpose, meaning and a life well lived. It is happiness. You no longer live in the past or the future. You will not dwell on past mistakes or regrets. You will not dwell for hours on what you should have done, or what could have happened. You will live in the present. You will not live in the future. You will not be thinking that you will be happy when you pass the next exam or get the next job or when you buy the dream home. You are grateful for all that you have. There is only the present. Happiness will not be a hope, a dream, or a goal to be pursued.

Gratitude has an energy that causes others to be drawn to you. It is a virtue with tremendous power that affects all with whom you come in contact. It has infinite motion, impacting in profound ways on what you do throughout the day, and the affect you have on others. As much as gratitude is something you own personally, it is shared with others, and infuses energy and optimism. Gratitude for all people and things propels you to reach out and be with others— being there for others as a healing agent in a broken world. It is virtue in motion, because no matter what the situation, you are grateful and motivated to move forward.

Your gratitude is a breathing and living sign of the person of love you have become. It is a virtue in motion because it empowers others. They experience the gratitude you have for them and the confidence you have in them. It lets others know that they are important and wanted and appreciated. It inspires them to act.

3. Wisdom

Wisdom and prudence stretch beyond a body of knowledge, beyond the intellect. It is the ability to take all that we have experienced and learned and apply it in making good judgements. To have a wealth of experiences and great knowledge is of no use if we cannot apply it in making sound judgments. With wisdom and prudence, your decisions will always be made in the best interest of others. You will have risen above any prejudices or opinions you hold, any personal agendas you may have, and will be a life that heals and benefits the individual, the community and society.

I once asked a missionary, who was loved by the people, if he would like to be the president of the country. He quickly replied, "No, because if I was president I wouldn't be able to get as much done." He recognized that, in his country, affecting change required doing the work he was doing. He could see that in this military-based country, which operated falsely as a democracy, no president could affect real change, as could a missionary. Although he had the love and loyalty of the people, he did not use that to acquire more power or a higher position. For him, in his situation, he made wise decisions with the best interest of others in mind.

No matter what our ministry or profession, once we lose sight of the importance of the moment, the importance of simple acts of love, the importance of the infinite energy and effect created in that moment of loving, we lose our ability to be truly happy. This missionary had the wisdom to see that. It wasn't about position or power. It was about serving and loving others.

Whether you are a Wall Street hedge-fund manager, the CEO of a company, a teacher, carpenter or a cleaner, every decision and action must be made with wisdom. When it is, every decision and action is done out of love and for the benefit of others. Wise decisions lead to loving actions, which result in the fulfillment of the true self.

Wisdom and prudence allow you to see in ways that others cannot. You will see that great minds and great ideas have often been put to rest by those who lack self-discipline or tenacity. You will have the self-discipline and determination to put your love into action and bring it to fruition. No matter how difficult achieving success may be, you will be steadfast and refuse to give up. A wise person knows what it takes to carry out their mission. They apply self-discipline to their life, and know the role that determination plays in being successful.

With wisdom and prudence also comes hope. You know that for anything wonderful to happen it takes time. You have the gift of patience, being willing to continue to do the wonderful work you do, living in the hope that healing will come to this broken world. You will not become frustrated and impatient, making hasty decisions or decisions based on emotions. You can see above and beyond, as if you stand above yourself, looking down on the world. You have perspective. Wisdom and prudence gives you the ability to see what others cannot.

A life without hope is a desperate life. With hope now in your life, you will look to tomorrow as another great opportunity, affecting change to make something wonderful happen. No matter how difficult today is, you will move forward in the faith of knowing that better times are ahead. You will live the active and ambitious life, creating a better world for everyone.

4. Empathy

Without getting into a lengthy discussion regarding the definitions and differences between empathy, sympathy and compassion, let us state that we include all three in this virtue. It is of no use, if one feels empathy for someone, but that empathy is not put into compassionate action. It only leads to emotional distress when it is bottled up. When we say that someone is empathetic, we mean that they are also compassionate. In this way, empathy is a virtue in motion, shown in compassionate acts that attempt to alleviate the suffering of others.

We know that we cannot get rid of all suffering, but we make the attempt, doing what we can, to alleviate suffering. There are those who are bed-ridden or those who suffer handicaps that make them immobile. This does not hinder their ability to put this virtue into action. Wishing well to others, treating all with kindness, saying prayers for those who suffer, are all ways that we can impact on the world outside of us, in an active way. Empathy is a great and powerful virtue in motion.

Sympathy and empathy allow you to understand and share another person's experiences and emotions, suffering with them. You will have great compassion and care for another because you see their suffering as your suffering. Your oneness with their suffering will move you to take action on their behalf.

We were all created equal in that we all desire happiness, and we deserve happiness. Everyone has a right to happiness.

Realizing that everyone has a right to happiness makes us more empathetic towards others and propels us to do what we can to bring about a state of happiness for them.

When we work at freeing others from the suffering they experience, we increase our own serenity, actualize our own gifts, fulfill our own purpose and thus, find happiness.

"The highest level of inner calm comes from the development of love and compassion. The more concerned we are with the happiness of others, the more we increase our own well-being." (Dalai Lama). Empathy tears down all the borders, conflicts and external forces that separate us. Empathy creates an understanding of our inter-connectedness and causes us to live it out. Our life is filled with opportunities, on every level, in our own career and through our everyday acts, to alleviate the economic, political, psychological, and emotional suffering of others.

Although you will experience suffering, you will taste a joy you have never known, found in your inter-connectedness with humanity and your love for all things. Although you will often be troubled because the suffering of others is your suffering, you will know peace. Although you will experience frailty and failure through your compassion, you will be lifted, and will lift others to great heights. This empathy is part of the meaning and purpose of your life, to work towards being a person for others.

It is important to note that empathy also gives us the ability to share in the success and joy of others. How wonderful it is to experience the success and joy of another person!

The temptation is to envy them, be jealous of them. Some actually wish harm to those who have great success or joy. Empathy allows us to feel and share their joy, and by so doing we motivate them to continue their journey of success and joy. We inspire others also to seek that success and joy when we are able to relish in the success of another. We fill the world with a positive energy that injects enthusiasm in others. The virtue of empathy is one of the most powerful virtues in motion.

5. Forgiveness

Forgiving another and showing mercy is considered to be one of life's most difficult challenges, especially when you were the victim of the offence. Great religious leaders, such as Jesus, make it clear that we cannot live a fruitful or happy life if we are unforgiving. They recognize how difficult it is to be forgiving, but make it clear that freedom is not possible without forgiveness.

Your new life will be one that is free of anger, hatred, and a desire for vengeance. In this newfound freedom, you are able to move forward in new and empowering ways, no longer tied to the past or to the victim mentality. By being merciful and forgiving, you will live in the present, acting in just and prudent ways and being a person for others. With mercy and forgiveness in your heart you are free to live out your true nature using the great talents and gifts you possess.

With mercy and forgiveness, we acquire other great virtues, such as cooperation, acceptance, and tolerance. You no longer allow the ego or the personal agendas of others to get in the way of working with them to accomplish the goal of the mission. You will actualize true teamwork with others, as well as with management. You will be a critical ingredient in making great and wonderful things happen.

My father received the Governor General's Award for heroism having overtaken an armed gunman who was holding up a gas station, and putting the gun to my father's head. Following a lot of grappling, and gunfire which grazed my father's abdomen and thigh, this 70-year-old retiree overtook the young bandit and held him peacefully to the ground.

When interviewed on radio and television, he expressed his sympathy for the young man, not holding any grudges or bad feelings and wished him well. His forgiveness was unconditional, complete, and true. In spite of many critical comments regarding my father's forgiving and empathetic heart towards this man, he stood true to forgiveness. I believe it was that forgiving heart that allowed my father to move forward in his life free of any anger, resentments, or trauma.

I have witnessed people forgiving their spouse for doing terrible things. Amazingly, in many cases, the perpetrator became a more loyal, loving, and faithful spouse than they could have ever been if they had not done wrong and had not received forgiveness. Forgiveness is a virtue in motion, transforming the heart, mind and actions of self and others. It is an infinite body of energy, exuded into the universe, which causes great change.

Truly, forgiveness is a powerful virtue in motion, for transforming lives.

Just as important as forgiving others is our ability to forgive ourselves. It is difficult to forgive oneself. It is often easier to forgive someone who has offended you than to forgive self.

I worked with many students who felt this way, even when there was nothing to forgive. Students who were victims of incest sometimes blamed themselves and found it easier to live with and forgive the parent than to forgive themselves. Students who went through a family divorce, or watched one of their parents carry on an adulterous relationship, sometimes blamed themselves and found it difficult to forgive themselves. Of course, in all these cases, the teens were not at fault in any way, but being able to forgive themselves was a challenging task.

Many of the youth I worked with who had committed terrible crimes like robbery, and in one case murder, found it almost unbearable to live with their guilt, and unable to forgive themselves. Whether the youth were responsible or not responsible, they sometimes saw themselves as unworthy of another's love. They couldn't love themselves so they didn't believe anyone would love them. The girl who suffered incest over a long period of time, and saw herself merely as an instrument of pleasure for her father, believed she was unlovable. She could not love herself.

I remember putting my hand on hers and saying to her, "You may find it hard to believe that people love you and that you are worthy of love, but *believe* that you are worthy of love. God loves you as his beautiful innocent child." She broke down and cried.

How wonderful and free is the life you now live, able to forgive others and to forgive yourself. You are free of playing a part in gossip, slander, bad feelings, anger, and any resentments.

You are free! This freedom allows those you forgive, and you yourself, to move forward, to live a full and flourishing life.

Forgiveness certainly is a powerful virtue in motion.

6. Charity

Your status and accomplishments will not be measured by your gold pens and oak desks, but instead by your willingness to care for and help those around you who are in need. You are no longer tied to wealth and power, a prisoner to society's yardstick of success. You will now live a prudent and generous life, sharing what you have with those in need. This will not lead to your impoverishment, but rather to your happiness and abundance.

Not only will you share financially, but you will be sharing your time, talents, and great abilities to effectively heal a broken world. You have heard it said, "how great a nation we are will be determined by how we treat our weakest members." By the same token, how great a person we are will be determined by how we treat the weakest people.

After returning from mission work in one of the Developing Countries I would be booked by a number of organizations to give presentations on the mission and their needs. When I presented to wealthy groups or organizations, I often left with a coffee mug as a gift of appreciation. When I presented to poor church congregations I would leave with a few thousand dollars in donations. I found it astonishing and inspiring to discover how the poor were more charitable than the rich.

I believe this charitable heart was a result of the gratitude they had, in spite of their meagre and difficult life. They clearly saw the inter-connectedness of humanity, and from this perspective they lived a life with purpose and meaning.

I counselled a young girl whose mother was a drug addict and prostitute. When the young girl reached the age of 13, her mother introduced her to this life to help pay for her addiction.

In addition, she had to live in squalor and was subject to a lot of abuse, including such things as drinking water from the toilet as a form of punishment. The girl left home as a teenager to make a life for herself. Occasionally she would see her mother working the streets. She had heard from others that her mother longed to see her. A few years had passed, and the teen visited her mother.

She accepted who her mother was. She had no aspirations of establishing a healthy relationship with her, but visited her because she felt sorry for her mother, and assumed that her forgiveness and visit would let her mother know that there were no hard feelings. This was a great act of charity, and it is charitable acts such as these that stand the best chance of changing the life of the recipient.

Generosity is much more than a sense of duty, like tithing. It is who we are, and it is a way of life. You do not give with a heavy heart or with worry. You give with enthusiasm.

Your enthusiasm will be infectious to all those who also seek to live a happy life. You will not be deterred and when your actions do not produce the yield you anticipated, you will continue with enthusiasm. This enthusiasm, expressing itself in the form of cheerfulness and energy, will be efficacious, creating what it symbolizes. It will spread, changing the hearts of others, and inspiring them to take the journey you have taken.

Having a charitable heart is more than being generous with your money. A person with a charitable heart gives with their time, their listening, their efforts, and their talents, all for the sake of another's well-being. A person with a charitable heart takes the time to visit the sick, call a lonely friend, listen to someone's heartache, share a talent. Such a person is generous and charitable in all ways.

7. Peacefulness

Peacefulness is an inner state of calm. Without peacefulness, there cannot be wisdom or the ability to see things clearly and make prudent decisions. Peacefulness generates a mind clear of preconceived ideas and the muddle of life. It causes a person to approach every situation, not with surrender but with acceptance. The thoughts and actions of a peaceful mind will seek justice but at the same time, will accept all things, including suffering. It is a virtue that affects great change in others through the ability to accept, and at the same time to make decisions and actions based on that which is just. In this way, it truly is a virtue in motion.

After studying Buddhism for some time, I thought I would put my father to the test. As I have already mentioned, I viewed him as being enlightened, living out the formula herein and exercising the eight virtues. I was fascinated by koans. These are riddles given to monks to test their progress towards enlightenment. It tests whether months of meditation and reflection has led to the emptying of one's mind of all the muddle, entrapments, and traditional ways of thinking.

For example, a monk was given this koan by his master: 'There is an egg placed at the bottom of a goose necked bottle. The duck hatches and begins to grow in the bottle until it is too large for its home. How do you get the duck out of the bottle?' The monk would report daily to his master with his answer. It is common for it to take two years before a monk arrives at an acceptable answer. They may come back with answers such as: cut off the top of the bottle, starve the duck until you can feed it through the neck, gently break the bottle. These answers are all unacceptable and the monk would return to meditation.

What is the problem with these answers? They reflect a muddled mind, trapped in the traditional ways of thinking.

Buddhism demands, just as this pilgrimage does, that you completely empty your mind of all things, so that you will have a peace-filled mind that can see clearly. Finally, after eighteen months, the monk delivered an acceptable answer. To the question, "How do you get the duck out of the bottle?" The monk answered, "There! It is out."

It is difficult for a western mind, such as mine, to see this as an acceptable answer. Perhaps the monk had shown that he had finally emptied his mind of traditional thought patterns.

Perhaps it demonstrated that he had freed himself of the walls and barriers, the prejudices and opinions that imprisoned him. Like him, the duck was free. It just was.

I decided to give my father a koan. My father was a simple man who didn't have any formal education, but who nevertheless found the happiness we speak of here, through his own methods. Having no knowledge of Buddhism or the concept of a koan, I explained to him that I was going to give him a riddle, and it was critical that he deliver back to me an immediate and spontaneous response.

I asked him, "If you know the sound of two hands clapping, what is the sound of one?" He immediately replied,

"Loneliness."

I was profoundly moved, as it further confirmed to me that he had emptied his mind of all the nonsense, and had acquired a peacefulness of mind that could see things this clearly. It is no wonder that his peacefulness, which affected the way he lived his life, impacted on the lives of so many others. People wanted to be in his company. They actually felt peaceful being next to him. Peacefulness is certainly a virtue in motion.

War is not living a life in motion; it is living a life in reverse. War moves us backward, thwarting human progress.

Living a life of peacefulness, internally and externally, is a life in real forward motion. Gandhi is proof of this. His non-violent approach changed the world, without him raising a fist. His capacity to love and his quest for inner and external peace allowed him to see the world as few can. His example allows us as individuals, as well as a society, to focus on that which creates greatness and to put it into action. Peacefulness creates real social change.

You now have the clarity and peacefulness of mind to overcome ignorance and make clear, prudent decisions. You now have the courage to do that which is frightening. You no longer swim upstream because you have the attitude of acceptance. You have strength in the face of pain or grief. You will be fearless and bold, knowing that what you are doing is for the good, and that good brings great joy. The old fears will no longer hinder you from acquiring truth and living a life of love.

You will have a non-violent active attitude motivated by

the wish to do good for others. You no longer react with abusive behavior or passive aggressive behavior when you don't get what you want. Your non-violent approach to all things becomes a way of life. Your mind is no longer clouded by feelings of anger.

Anger no longer impedes on your ability to practice reason. With your peacefulness will come friendliness and kindness. Others will desire your company and friendship.

Your friendliness and warmth will be the magnet that draws others to you. Your congeniality and affection will create in them a desire to have what you have. Your open-door approach and kindness will inspire others to go on the journey you traveled.

8. Integrity

With integrity comes self-esteem. You know that your words and actions are truthful, and you are a person of integrity.

When you know this about yourself, you never doubt what a wonderful person you are. Knowing that you are at your Core, a being of love, and that living out that love will bring you true happiness.

You will derive a feeling of deep satisfaction in the good works you do, and with the accomplishments you make, great and small. Your life will be filled with purpose and meaning, healing and elevating others to higher ground. You will feel good about yourself and the life you live, taking great pride in a job well done.

It was an honor to spend time with Father John Boca in Rwanda. He is a Cambodian priest who has a mission in Central America. When I met him he was visiting the poor village he grew up in. He went back to the church where his entire family of seven were slaughtered. I asked him if he was mad at God. He said, "God does not carry a gun. Man does. God gives us hands and arms to work, to create, to love. We choose to carry guns.

There is hunger in the world because man administers God's gifts unequally and there is violence because man chooses to abuse God's gifts." With integrity, we will use the gifts we have been given, always for the righteous cause. We live our life doing that which brings honor to ourselves and others, and not pleasure or gratification from primitive emotions such as power, revenge, or jealousy.

I have worked for leaders who were so political that any decision they made escaped rational thought and was detrimental to the individual or the community. However, it was politically correct. This lack of integrity impacted negatively on the development and excellence of themselves and the community. Whenever I worked for leaders who had great integrity, unwilling to compromise what they believed to be true, the communities flourished, exemplifying excellence in every area.

Integrity in motion is a powerful tool, transforming individuals and communities. If one always operates out of integrity, whether they are right or wrong, individuals and communities fair better.

TECHNIQUE

We are unable to achieve perfect happiness but, as we discussed, we can find complete happiness. Bycomplete, we mean a life of happiness with which we are content. Now that we have arrived at this point, we want to avoid falling back into old ways. To maintain and foster this state of liberation and enlightenment, we need to adopt a technique to be used throughout our everyday lives. Many world religions promote lengthy meditation or prayer. Some encourage active participation in church community and rituals. Some modern-day self-help techniques will promote journaling or adopting specific programs. All of these are effective ways to get where you want to go and to maintain the place you are in.

The technique I offer for this program is a bit different.

The technique I offer is threefold. First, every day we recite the three promises we have made to ourselves. Although we have completed the pilgrimage and achieved complete happiness, we must recite these three promises daily to remain in the state we are in.

Secondly, in re-stating these promises we continually make the effort to overcome ego, fear, social pressures, and the desire to seek comfort. We seek to always be emptying ourselves to be born anew.

Thirdly, throughout the day, we remind ourselves of the eight virtues and the way we respond in each situation to actualize those virtues.

Before we discuss an issue with our spouse or friend, we remind ourselves to be humble and grateful. Prior to entering a job interview, we will remind ourselves that we will have integrity. Prior to a meeting or a conversation with a stranger, we remind ourselves of our empathy. Before we go to sleep at night, we remind ourselves of our compassion. As we awake, we remind ourselves to practice empathy and forgiveness that day.

When we are about to do a job, we remind ourselves that we will be patient and truthful in our work. Before we approach a conflict, we remind ourselves that we will promote peacefulness.

These constant reminders are just reminders of what we already are, and what we have become, but they also serve as a point of clarity and practice. We become, in motion, that which we repeatedly practice. Even the Buddha and Jesus, after achieving enlightenment, spent hours every day in prayer or meditation. Doing this brings clarity of thought and the strength required not to fall back into our old ways.

It may sound rather arduous to live out these three practices throughout the day, but it is not. We are not spending hours a day meditating in the lotus position. We are spending
moments throughout the day reminding ourselves of the promises we made, doing a spiritual check on our state of mind, and determining how we can put into motion the eight virtues.

This will not take copious amounts of time, only brief moments throughout the day. When these three exercises become habits, we find that if we stop to reflect, our mind and spirit will crave to do them. We will, in a sense, become addicted to them. It will just become a part of who we are and what we do.

I offer here another technique you may want to employ. It requires your input. Each day you may want to remind yourself of the virtues you now live. It would be helpful if you recite these daily. It will be your own personal plan. I have listed one statement for each. You may want to add two of your own commitments to each virtue:

1. Humility:
A. I will listen to all people, including the voice of a child, in the hope of learning something new and wonderful.
B.
C.

2. Gratitude:
A. I am grateful for all things, even my suffering, because it will forge greatness within me.
B.
C.

3. Wisdom:
A. I will avoid popular thought for the sake of knowing that which is true.
B.
C.

4. Empathy:
A. I will see others as my brothers and sisters, their suffering being my suffering, their joy my joy.
B.
C.

5. Forgiveness:
A. I will forgive those who have offended me and forgive myself for my own misgivings.
B.
C.

6. Charity:
A. I will be generous in all ways; with my financial resources, time, energy, and the gifts I possess.
B.
C.

7. Peacefulness:

A. I will, in thought, word and action approach every person and every situation with a calm mind and peacefulness.

B.

C.

8. Integrity:

A. At home, at work and at play I will always be true to myself and never compromise my integrity.

B.

C.

THE NEW YOU

Congratulations! You have completed the journey.

By reaching the Core, you will live out the virtues and as a result be a great healer and elevator of others. Never underestimate your healing power. You have the ability to accomplish great things. Never underestimate the powerful and rippling effect of your simple acts of love. You now live in oneness with the highest level of your being. A level that exists above and beyond the senses and cognitive thought. You live in union with the Divine. You will live out your full potential.

You now live a life through the real self, the virtuous self.

Living a life for others, a life of healing. Now empowered, stable, confident, self-assured, calm, in harmony and enlightened, you will live what you are called to be, an instrument of healing in a broken world, elevating others to higher ground. In living this life based on truth, cloaked in love, and expressed through the virtues, you will live a purpose filled, meaningful life and will have found true happiness.

www.ingramcontent.com/pod-product-compliance
Lightning Source LLC
Chambersburg PA
CBHW071101120626
46546CB00003B/1241